BY ROBERT D. KAPLAN

EARNING
THE
ROCKIES

RANDOM HOUSE

NEW YORK

EARNING THE ROCKIES

HOW GEOGRAPHY SHAPES AMERICA'S ROLE IN THE WORLD

—

ROBERT D. KAPLAN

Copyright © 2017 by Robert D. Kaplan

Map copyright © 2017 by David Lindroth Inc.

All rights reserved.

Published in the United States by Random House,
an imprint and division of Penguin Random House LLC, New York.

RANDOM HOUSE and the HOUSE colophon are registered
trademarks of Penguin Random House LLC.

LIBRARY OF CONGRESS CATALOGING-IN-PUBLICATION DATA
NAMES: Kaplan, Robert D., author.
TITLE: Earning the Rockies : how geography shapes America's
role in the world / Robert D. Kaplan.
DESCRIPTION: New York : Random House, [2017] |
Includes bibliographical references and index.
IDENTIFIERS: LCCN 2016013488 | ISBN 9780399588211
(alk. paper) | ISBN 9780399588235 (ebook)
SUBJECTS: LCSH: United States—Geography. | United States—Description
and travel. | Kaplan, Robert D.—Travel—United States. | Landscapes—
Social aspects—United States. | City and town life—United States. |
United States—Social conditions—1980– | United States—Territorial expansion. |
Imperialism—History. | National characteristics, American. |
United States—Foreign relations—Philosophy.
CLASSIFICATION: LCC E161.3 .K37 2017 | DDC 306.097309/048—dc23
LC record available at https://lccn.loc.gov/2016013488

Printed in the United States of America on acid-free paper

randomhousebooks.com

246897531

First Edition

Title-page images © iStock

Book design by Barbara M. Bachman

To

WILLIAM WHITWORTH

Vaulting the sea, the prairies' dreaming sod,
Unto us lowliest sometimes sweep, descend
And of the curveship lend a myth to God.

—HART CRANE, *"To Brooklyn Bridge,"* *1930*

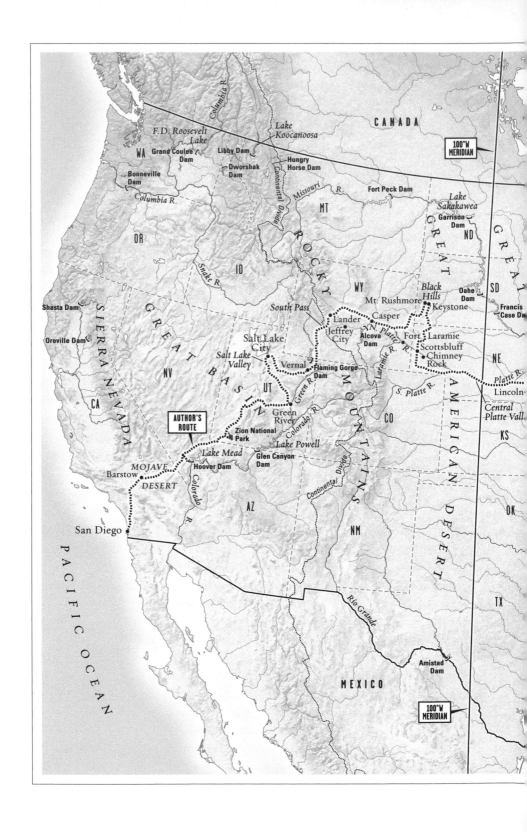

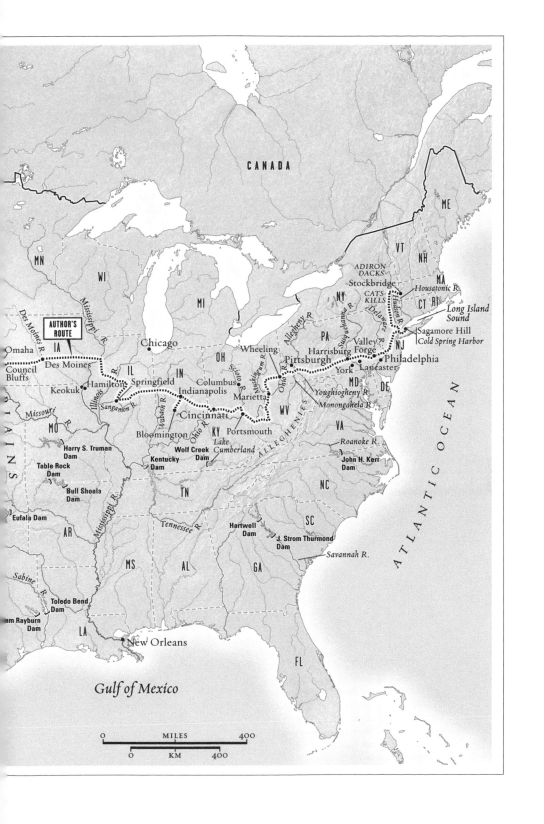

CANADA

MN
WI
MI
CHICAGO
IA
Omaha
Council Bluffs
Des Moines
Keokuk
Hamilton
Springfield
Bloomington
Indianapolis
Cincinnati
Columbus
Marietta
Portsmouth
Wheeling
Pittsburgh
Harrisburg
Valley Forge
Philadelphia
Lancaster
York

AUTHOR'S ROUTE

Des Moines R.
Mississippi R.
Illinois R.
Sangamon R.
Wabash R.
Ohio R.
Scioto R.
Muskingum R.
Allegheny R.
Susquehanna R.
Delaware R.
Hudson R.
Youghiogheny R.
Monongahela R.

ADIRON-DACKS
Stockbridge
CATS-KILLS
Housatonic R.
Long Island Sound
Sagamore Hill
Cold Spring Harbor

ME
VT
NH
MA
CT
RI
NY
PA
NJ
MD
DE
OH
IN
IL

Missouri R.
MO
Harry S. Truman Dam
Table Rock Dam
Bull Shoals Dam
Eufala Dam
AR
Sabine R.
Toledo Bend Dam
am Rayburn Dam
LA
New Orleans

Wolf Creek Dam
Kentucky Dam
Lake Cumberland
KY
TN
Tennessee R.
Hartwell Dam
J. Strom Thurmond Dam
MS
AL
GA
SC
NC
VA
WV
ALLEGHENIES
Roanoke R.
John H. Kerr Dam
Savannah R.

FL

ATLANTIC OCEAN

Mississippi R.

Gulf of Mexico

0   MILES   400
0   KM   400

CONTENTS

INVOCATION

To use the words of the poet William Carlos Williams, the object is to describe a giant—the United States—*out of particulars:*[1] in this case, a father's memories of travel, a historian's geography of hope, a desert of biblical proportions, and an ocean advancing toward China. The father provides the inspiration; the historian the necessary and operable myth; the desert the challenge that must be met, without which other challenges cannot be met; the ocean the path to Cathay, that is, the path toward obligations in the outer world—and the giant's eventual dissolution in it—all of which follow from the original conquest of a continent.

EARNING
THE
ROCKIES

The author's father, pictured on the left.

COURTESY OF THE AUTHOR

EARNING THE ROCKIES

IF I DON'T REMEMBER MY FATHER'S NAME, WHO WILL?

My father's name was Philip Alexander Kaplan. He was born in Brooklyn in 1909. I don't recall him ever at peace with his life. I do remember him looking serene once at Valley Forge, among the oaks and maples and magnolias; clustered among the numerous birches and pine trees; and a second time among other hardwoods at Fredericksburg. These are trees I could not name when I was young but learned to identify on later visits to those hallowed sites, and to other sites on the Eastern Seaboard that the memory of my father inspired me to see. For it was only at such places, away from our immediate surroundings, that my father became real to me, and real to himself.

In particular, I remember him at Wheatland, James Buchanan's handsome Federal-style home with the air of a southern plantation in Lancaster, Pennsylvania. There I peeked my chin over the protective barriers into sumptuous mid-nineteenth-century rooms, with their dark walnut desks and other antique furniture, along with the French china, glittering crystal, and gilded mirrors. Yes, I remember a grand piano there and many shadowy bookcases and lithographs. For long spans of my childhood my memory is vague, but it lights up with minute detail about what matters most to me. Wheatland, where President Buchanan lived, worked, headquartered his campaign for high office, and died, really mattered to me as a child. I was only nine, but my father in those rare moments spoke to me almost as though I were an adult, even as he was so full of tenderness.

My father laid out the fundamentals of Buchanan's failure as president, perhaps the worst in our history: a story necessarily simplified for a nine-year-old. Of course, later in life I would fill in most of the details.

Whatever the multitude of factors in the three-way election of 1856, James Buchanan was by no means an accidental president. When he assumed office in March 1857, he appeared to have everything going for him. Arguably, no man in the country was better qualified for the task of calming the festering North-South split over slavery. He was a tall, reasonably wealthy, self-made, and imposing figure, someone who, aside from being a bachelor, was truly good at life: a former congressman, senator, minister to Russia in the Andrew Jackson administration, secretary of state in the James K. Polk administration, and minister to Great Britain in the Franklin Pierce administration; a talented and accomplished operator, a man of maneuver gifted at the fine art of compromise despite his stubbornness. He knew what buttons to push, in other words. *Who else was possessed of the political savvy necessary to save the Union?* Few were shrewder. Except for one thing, as it would turn out: Buchanan did not have a compass point toward which to navigate in the midst of all the deals he tried to make, and he had a distinct and fatal sympathy for the South. But mostly he was all ambition and technique without direction. Moreover, he was a literalist. He had a small vision of the Constitution and the frontier nation: he did not believe he and the federal government had the right to dictate terms to the southern states. He saw the good in both the pro-slavery and anti-slavery points of view. With his legalistic flair, he might have made a very competent president in more ordinary times; he was a disaster in extraordinary times. The country finally came apart under his watch. "It turned out, he just, *ehhh,* didn't have what it takes," a father whispered to a nine-year-old boy at Wheatland.

The basic security of the world in the twentieth and early twenty-first centuries has depended greatly upon the political unity of the temperate zone of North America. And that almost didn't happen. It was my knowledge of both Buchanan's many gifts and his abject personal failure as president—a knowledge first granted me by my father—that provided me with a deeper awareness of just how difficult making epochal decisions in the moment of crisis can be. It was this very awareness about Buchanan—how good he looked at the beginning of his administration and how bad he turned out—that always made me think later in life, *Thank God we had Lincoln.* What Buchanan ultimately lacked, despite his résumé, Lincoln had in abundance: character.

But Buchanan's failure was secondary in my father's eyes that day at Wheatland; primary was the fact that Buchanan was, nevertheless, part of the vital tapestry of American history. Therefore, he was well worth knowing about. Great presidents cannot be understood in isolation; one requires knowledge of the not-great presidents who preceded and succeeded them. Indeed, we need always to see history as a whole, we cannot appreciate the good without knowing the bad, and vice versa. This is especially true of westward expansion. Wheatland made America's past come alive for me.

IT WAS AT A HOTEL in Lancaster during that same trip that my parents bought me a volume of American travel articles written in easy *Reader's Digest* style, suited to my age. One story was about a family driving west and stopping for breakfast at a diner somewhere in Nebraska perhaps, on the Great Plains (or the Great American Desert as it was once known), anticipating the sight of the Rocky Mountains, where they were headed. "You have to earn the Rockies," the father says to his wife and children, in my piercing if inaccurate childhood recollection of the story, by driving across the flat Midwest and Plains. Perhaps it was "meet the challenge of the Rockies." In any case, *earn the Rockies* is a phrase that has stayed with me my whole life. It sums up America's continental geography, the continent that Lincoln united and realized, and the significance of the Rocky Mountains as a geographical fact that should only be encountered by first crossing the Eastern Seaboard, the Middle West, and the Great American Desert, for that was the way that they were encountered in all their sudden and terrifying magnificence by European settlers and pathfinders, those who could not have known what exactly lay over the horizon.

Throughout my childhood I yearned to see mountains higher than the Appalachians. As a family, we never left the eastern states. The Rockies were just too far, and my parents simply lacked the means, though my father talked about them often. The phrase *earn the Rockies* helped spur me to travel, something also instilled in me by my father since I can remember.

My mother and father took me on that trip through Pennsylvania in 1962. Alaska and Hawaii had only recently been admitted to the Union. The United States back then, for a while yet, still thought of itself as only a continental nation, stretching, according to both the song and the cliché, from sea to shining sea. To this day, Alaskans refer to the rest of the country as "the Lower 48," meaning the contiguous forty-eight states that constitute the temperate zone of North America. Arizona was the last of the Lower 48, admitted to the Union only in 1912, a little closer in time to that trip through Pennsylvania than that trip through Pennsylvania was to the moment at which I write.

America was a different country then, vaster and emptier. Valley Forge was not in the suburbs of Greater Philadelphia as it is now, nor Fredericksburg near the suburbs of Greater Washington, D.C. Food was more distinctive—with far fewer chain restaurants and grits widespread in eating facilities just south of the nation's capital. People drove and rode buses, or hitchhiked across America—as I did in the summer of 1970—much more often than they flew. The Interstate Highway System was spanking new, and thus the Pennsylvania Turnpike and New York State Thruway constituted exotic experiences, with rest stops offering sit-down dining with waiters and waitresses. Those magical highways could transport you from the Atlantic Seaboard all the way to the very rim of the Midwest! The East Coast was much more of an adventure then than it is now. And there were few crowds anywhere.

It had its dark side, though. I remember stopping for lunch with my parents at a restaurant called Lowery's in Tappahannock, Virginia. It was the spring of 1964, just a few months before the Civil Rights Act, and we were returning north from a visit to the Yorktown Battlefield. There was a sign at the entrance as we opened the door: "Whites Only." I saw my parents look uneasily at each other, something that communicated fear to an eleven-year-old boy. We went inside, ate quietly, and noticed everyone glancing at us. It was clear that we were not locals and therefore not entirely welcome.

Those trips were the gemstones of my childhood. It is in the midst of recalling them that I cherish the memory of my parents the most. Returning from those trips I was able to see, as though a shocked outsider, the grainy, almost black-and-white surroundings of our home in Queens: the sooty fire escape and other blockhouse apartments were the only view from the stifling kitchen where we ate. Because of the clash between where we had been and where we lived, those early travels, I believe, burdened me with something I was never entirely comfortable with: a cruel objectivity. In the morning we had been at Wheatland seeing the feast of glittering greenery outside James Buchanan's mansion; that same night we were back in our apartment, hearing the yelling of our neighbors in other apartments. Seeing the wider world, if only a glimpse of it, had come with a price. I learned early that comparison is painful and not always polite, but it is at the root of all serious analysis.

My father was a truck driver with a high school education who listened to classical music on WQXR while breezing through the *New York Times* Sunday and weekday crossword puzzles. He had a small record collection that included the patriotic band music of John Philip Sousa and the hits of Al Jolson, mixed with a little Stephen Foster. It was music that took you from the mid-nineteenth century to the first decades of the twentieth, telegraphing the country's latent dynamism as it crept toward World War II. There was also in this singular and awkward repertoire the haunting twangs of Ferde Grofé's *Grand Canyon Suite* from 1931, with their hopeful intimations of travel. In the 1960s, my father was decades behind his time. As I grew into middle age, I realized how grateful I was for it.

In the spring of 1961, my father took my family, including my older brother and a cousin, on a trip to Washington, D.C. It was particularly memorable because on the second night he got us tickets to hear the Marine Band play Sousa at Constitution Hall. Between such transformative moments—Wheatland, the Marine Band—was the weeping undertow of my childhood: every late afternoon, my father, hunched over the unmade bed that was visible from the windows of apartment houses directly across, tying the laces on his work boots, lost briefly in a trance, preparing for another night of driving in the partial wasteland of Brooklyn. Facing him in the bedroom was his small collection of books, two shelves actually. I remember *The Conquest of Everest* by Sir John Hunt (1954),

Beyond the High Himalayas by William O. Douglas (1952), *Jefferson the Virginian* by Dumas Malone (1948), and one he had just bought, and that he anticipated reading: *Travels with Charley: In Search of America* by John Steinbeck (1962).

In the 1930s my father had spent his twenties riding railway cars around the United States, earning a living as a horse-racing tout in forty-three of the lower forty-eight states. After a "big score" he would check into a first-class hotel, a large cigar in hand: twenty-four hours later, he would be living a hobo's existence like so many others in the 1930s. He filled me with stories of his escapades in Depression-era America, and of the predominant image of a still-pastoral and naïve nation, where the scams he ran were relatively innocent and people bought you a meal when you were down and out. I have a picture of him, powerful in the way of a photo negative, with a jacket and tie and sharp fedora, wearing a confident smile with which I could never associate him when I was a child, taken at the Texas State Fair in Dallas: the year "1933" emblazoned above him.

Beulah Park (Columbus, Ohio), Arlington Downs (Dallas–Fort Worth), Churchill Downs, where he watched Bold Venture win the Kentucky Derby in 1936—my father knew literally every racetrack in the country. There were Houston and New Orleans in the winter of 1933–34; by freight train (the Union Pacific) from Pittsburgh to Chicago to Las Vegas the following year; sick, broke, back on his feet. It was an epic existence, however aimless, seedy, and pathetic at the edges, as well as full of exaggeration in the telling.

My father's last memory of travel was in 1942. He had just completed basic training at Fort Polk, Louisiana, and was heading north on a troop train for dispatch to Europe, where he would serve in the U.S. Army Eighth Air Force in England. At a rail junction near Cairo, Illinois, the sun was setting in rich colors over the prairie. Other trains were then converging from several tracks onto a single line that would take the troops to points along the East Coast, where ships to Europe awaited. Across a wide arc, the only thing he saw were trains and more trains, with soldiers looking out through every window as each train curved toward the others against a flat and limitless landscape lit red by the sun. "Just looking at that scene, that's the moment when I knew we were going to win the war," he said to me, smiling briefly at the recollection as he completed tying his shoelaces.

My first map of the United States was composed of my father's images. It was a landscape full of lessons and marvels that I desperately wanted to experience firsthand. The flat prairie was something I never imagined as dull but, rather, as an immense and magnificent prelude to something grander. I thank my father for that. And thus I would make several journeys from coast to coast: once in my late teens, hitchhiking, fueled with curiosity, obsessed with just seeing the West; then as a middle-aged journalist, writing about social, regional, and environmental issues; and now, finally, in my middle sixties, somewhat chastened by international events, hoping to learn something about America's place in the world by simply looking at the country around me.

Between those first and second trips I discovered an appropriate literary guide, a guide who saw intangibles written into the landscape similar to the ones my father had. Now I must reacquaint myself with his books in order to prepare for this next and likely final trip. Understanding America's situation can be a matter of rediscovering what is vital, yet forgotten; what is commonplace, yet overlooked. And with such books in hand, the American landscape itself beckons, underneath the convenient deceptions of the jet age. For the answers to our dilemmas overseas lie within the continent itself.

© BETTMANN/GETTY IMAGES

A CONTINENTAL EMPIRE

H E WAS A HOMER IN HIS WAY, RECALLING AS IF BY MEMORY WITH his eyes half closed a sacred past. He captured nation-state America at dead center: from his vantage point of World War II looking back a hundred years to the settlement of the American West. He did it with his own language, a true American idiom: consciously colorful, without being purple, like a good yarn told around a campfire by the last free men below the Tetons, "in the illimitable silence of the mountain night," as he had once put it.[1] Both the Left and Right at various moments would hate Bernard DeVoto, but within his rugged, twangy, unapologetic prose, buttressed by research in the Harvard library and the experience of a Utah boyhood, there is the sense in his writing that *this is how it really was.*

My father's youthful memories, oases in the midst of his sad and humiliating adulthood, encouraged me to discover the geo-

graphical wonders of my own country: one of the handful of inspi-
rations I could salvage from a dreary youth. Bernard De Voto was
the one who taught me how to think about those geographical
wonders. And by helping me to understand the American experience as a function of geography, De Voto would help me understand America's function in the wider world. I discovered De Voto
by accident in a bookstore in Boston in the early 1990s, after which
I was immediately swept up in the writer's narrative flourish that
was in keeping with my father's own enthusiasm, and own vision,
about the American West. De Voto became a pivotal figure for the
way I look at America, and by extension the world. He, more so
than other writers, taught me that America's first empire was not
in the Caribbean or more famously in the Philippines, but earlier,
in the American West itself. And that imperial legacy spoke about
patience and limits, rather than just about expansion.

Because De Voto is so critical to the way I see the American
continent and its fate in relation to the rest of the globe in the
twenty-first century, it is necessary that I describe his work in some
detail. Rereading his work constituted preparation, albeit indirect,
for this final journey: from one seaboard to the other.

BERNARD AUGUSTINE DE VOTO, born in Ogden, Utah, in 1897,
studied at the University of Utah and Harvard and later became a
columnist for *Harper's* for twenty years, until his death in 1955.
De Voto was the lyrical historian of westward expansion, devoting
his literary life to the subject, especially during the darkest days of
the 1940s when he employed the geopolitics of Manifest Destiny

as a means to tell Americans how not to despair. He was undoubt-edly a romantic, not in the way of a booster or propagandist, but rather as an area expert, somewhat in the erudite and sensuous manner of a Patrick Leigh Fermor or Lawrence Durrell. DeVoto demonstrated that the Rockies are deserving of the same exquisite, love-of-subject treatment as regions like the Balkans and Central Europe. In his classic *The Year of Decision: 1846,* published in 1942, DeVoto has a chapter, "*Anabasis* in Homespun," about the trek of the First Missouri Mounted Volunteers across 3,500 miles of prai-rie, desert, and mountain from Fort Leavenworth, Kansas, to the Rio Grande by way of Santa Fe, New Mexico, during the Mexican War. It is a trek that he ever so faintly compares to the "march up" of Xenophon's army of ten thousand Greek mercenaries from Mesopotamia across Anatolia and back to Greece 2,400 years ago. In both ancient Greece and nineteenth-century America, democ-racy is not merely some theoretical or philosophical construct but the organic reaction to an epic ordeal that is argued about by indi-vidual soldiers each night under the moon. This is Greek classical studies transported to the American frontier, written, as Wallace Stegner once remarked about his friend, with "gusto" and a "sense of participation" in history.[2]

DeVoto wrote about westward expansion less than a century after it had actually transpired—at a time when the East Coast elite still focused on its own country to a degree it doesn't anymore. Thus, he was not consigned to being a mere *regional* writer, but was a historian of the first rank. As Stegner says, DeVoto's *The Year of Decision: 1846* was a "declaration of national unity in time of crisis," completed just as the tide was turning at the Battle of Midway.[3]

DeVoto intuited deep in his bones, perhaps better than anyone else before or since, that the conquest of the Great Plains and the Rockies had been a necessary prelude in order to defeat the Nazis and the Japanese. And yet at the same time, his aversion to triumphalism allows him to approvingly quote Ralph Waldo Emerson on the tragedy of the Mexican War: "The United States will conquer Mexico but it will be as the man swallows the arsenic which brings him down in turn."[4] DeVoto, while celebrating the American expansionist impulse, throughout his narratives dependably recognizes the moral ambiguity of it.

DeVoto never once left the soil of North America. "As a historian," he wrote, "I have interested myself in the growth among the American people of the feeling that they were properly a single nation between two oceans; in the development of what I have called the continental mind."[5] This made him, above all, a man of maps. "He spread them on the floor of our living room," remembers the historian and biographer Catherine Drinker Bowen, "and we crawled from map to map, with Benny talking, until our knees were sore and our minds enlarged with names like Ogallala, Little Blue, Three Forks, Elephant Butte, the country of the Mandans, the Arikaras, and the Blackfeet."[6] Yet rather than being an American nativist who was uninterested in the rest of the world, DeVoto, according to the historian Arthur M. Schlesinger, Jr., was a radical idealist. "Nothing does greater credit to DeVoto's intelligence," Schlesinger writes, "than the clarity with which he saw the meaning of fascism. His character and concerns—his absorbing interest in the American past, his refusal ever to travel outside the American continent, his impatience with European examples and analogies—might well have predisposed him toward isolationism. But he had no doubt from the start either about American stakes in the war or about American responsibilities to the world."[7]

Schlesinger explains, "In that eerie twilight period between the invasion of Poland and Pearl Harbor, De Voto never faltered in the trenchancy of his perceptions. 'What ought they to say?' De Voto wrote of the presidential candidates in November 1940 [thirteen months before Pearl Harbor]. 'Simple, elementary, readily understandable things. . . . Just that the world is on fire. That America will be burned up unless you come awake and do something.'"[8]

And so it was that isolationists across America accused De Voto of "hysteria."[9]

Despite his love for the continental interior, De Voto, Stegner adds, "was almost offended by how *safe*" that same interior felt, "how snug and secure behind" their "lawns and banks of flowers" the Americans of the heartland were, even as Europe was suffering the onslaught of barbarians; so much so that De Voto "warned the Middle West about its smugness and isolationism." These warnings came in the course of a summer 1940 road trip across the United States, remembered fondly by De Voto's traveling companion, the young Schlesinger, fresh from a postgraduate year at the University of Cambridge in England. It was De Voto who mentored Schlesinger and taught him how the geography of the American West freighted the United States with a precise and unprecedented international destiny. De Voto saw dynamic, westering America, in Schlesinger's words, as "the redeemer, spreading its free institutions to less fortunate peoples."[10] De Voto was a humanitarian interventionist without the need of any moral philosophy. And he came to that conclusion by observing and meditating upon the continental landscape. He was foremost a listener. The soil of the American West taught him all he needed to know.

"DeVoto was not a cloistered scholar," writes the late Stephen E. Ambrose. "He got out on the trail, by foot, on horseback, and by canoe. He traveled where his characters had gone, seeing what they saw, listening to what they had said, and arguing for the conservation of their world."[11] DeVoto was an environmentalist before his time, out of a deep love of the American past more than out of an aesthetic love of the planet. For DeVoto this historical landscape of the West was liberating, for it was westward expansion into the Great Plains that defeated slavery (because the water-starved Great American Desert could not support a cotton culture). How sad it is that this man, this winner of the Pulitzer Prize and National Book Award—the very epitome of a liberal internationalist and environmentalist—who in his last years struck up a rich and penetrating friendship with Adlai Stevenson, even as he waged intellectual war against J. Edgar Hoover and the red-baiting Senator Joseph McCarthy, is, incredible as it may seem now, no longer read. Alas, in post–Vietnam War academic circles, the tendency to reduce American history to the crimes of slavery and "genocide" has simply left no room for DeVoto's vivid, solidly researched, fullbodied re-creation of the nineteenth-century American West.

Just as my father was usefully behind the times, so was DeVoto.

DEVOTO BEGINS HIS GREATEST and most essential book, *The Year of Decision: 1846,* with a quote from Henry David Thoreau: "Eastward

I go only by force; but westward I go free. . . . I must walk toward Oregon, and not toward Europe."[12]

Oregon, in this context, refers to the Oregon Territory, which includes the present-day states of Oregon, Washington, Idaho, and parts of Montana and Wyoming. To walk in that direction, in the sense that both DeVoto and Thoreau meant it, was not to turn inward and parochial, the way it might be perceived today, but to walk toward progress and freedom and away from the hatreds and constraints of the Old World: 1846 was the year that put America firmly on that path. It was the year when a one-term president, James Knox Polk, basically conceived and connived the doubling of the size of the United States, bringing into the fold of the Union the lands lying more or less west of the 1803 Louisiana Purchase: the Oregon Territory, California, Texas, and "New Mexico," as they were then known, thus conquering the Great American Desert.

Who was James K. Polk, or "Young Hickory" as he was called? DeVoto sets about answering in his typical rousing style. For despite his geographical raptures, he was always aware of how personalities shape history:

> He had been [Andrew] Jackson's mouthpiece and floor leader in the House of Representatives . . . had risen to the Speakership, had been governor of Tennessee. But sometimes the belt line shapes an instrument of use and precision. Polk's mind was rigid, narrow, obstinate, far from first-rate. He sincerely believed that only Democrats were truly American, Whigs being either the dupes or the pensioners of England. . . . He was pompous, suspicious, and se-

cretive; he had no humor; he could be vindictive; and he saw spooks and villains. He was a representative Southern politician of the second or intermediate period (which expired with his Presidency), when the decline but not the disintegration had begun.

But if his mind was narrow, it was also powerful and he had guts. If he was orthodox, his integrity was absolute and he could not be scared, manipulated, or brought to heel. No one bluffed him. . . . Furthermore, he knew how to get things done, which is the first necessity of government, and he knew what he wanted done, which is the second.

DeVoto states flatly that Polk's one term from 1845 to 1849 constituted "as strenuous an administration as any before Lincoln's." And between Andrew Jackson and Abraham Lincoln, James K. Polk was the only strong president, when the White House ruled instead of Congress. "That," says DeVoto, "is who James K. Polk was."[13]

Polk's knowledge of the West, though "thin and inaccurate," was nevertheless quite up to the task, given the logic of a continental, temperate-zone geography; the obstinacy with which he pursued that logic; and the ineffable energy of a westering people, who, again, owing to the forces of geography, loved the West before they had even seen it.[14] It is that energy in particular that *The Year of Decision: 1846* concerns itself with. DeVoto is a master of national and cultural essences, even as he is careful to anchor those essences in specific examples and thus avoid stereotyping. Manifest Destiny may have been raw and cruel and rapacious, but it was also an undeniable historical movement, as well as a definable mood of the times. And without it, obviously, the United States would simply have been unable to achieve what it did in the twentieth century in Europe and Asia.

Early on, DeVoto's wide-angle panorama on America in 1846 zooms in on a minute particular—the music of Stephen Foster. "A hundred years after him you need only play the opening bars of 'My Old Kentucky Home' or 'The Old Folks at Home' to stir in any American the full nostalgia of things past or to bind any audience, be it naturalized Czechs or the Daughters of the American Revolution, South Carolina Consistory, in the unity of a nation that knows itself." His point is that between the America of the 1840s and that of the 1940s, when DeVoto wrote, exists an almost insurmountable psychological barrier. The America of the 1840s did not think tragically in the way that the America of the 1940s did. Walt Whitman's poetry was certainly not tragic, and Nathaniel Hawthorne's work constituted not so much tragedy as melancholy. Herman Melville's *Moby-Dick* was still just over the horizon, and it would not impact the culture for decades to come. The devastation of the Civil War still lay in the future; the moral tragedy of the Mexican War was only just about to commence. Truly, the modern sensibility, in which doubt is the consequence of loss in a literal belief in God, had not quite arrived. The 1840s were still an era of great camp meetings, and the surest emotional pathway into that period is through Stephen Foster's songs—Susanna's "immortal quickstep," Jeanie with her light brown hair, the Camptown races, and so forth. While the America of the 1840s was divided by racial and sectional cleavages, as DeVoto writes, it also manifested a "commonality of feeling" that was as simple as it was genuine. We were "a forthright people, with a readiness of sincere tears and an energy that could be neither measured nor stayed."[15] These people were about to fight an "unpremeditated war" in Mexico and at the same time to build new homes in the West, an enterprise that had its horrors, petty jealousies, and even genocidal instincts. Stephen Foster's catchy and haunting rhythms were the background music to this burst of vitality and dynamism.

DeVoto moves on to the life of the mountain man James Clyman, who was born in 1792 in Fauquier County, Virginia, during the administration of George Washington, "on a farm that belonged to the President, whom he saw in the flesh." Clyman died "on his ranch at Napa, California, in 1881, during the administration of Chester Arthur. Jim Clyman was a man who went west," DeVoto thumps.[16] This is how he writes about geography: through individuals as well as through those vast, impersonal forces. Clyman's adventurous life leads to a discussion about the solitude and dangers of the Rocky Mountains, with their Indian war bands and lack of water, that would prove an even greater barrier to expansion than the solitude and dangers of the eastern forest and the prairie. The American character of today is still to some extent a frontier character born of those solitudes. Our rapacious form of capitalism, as well as the natural, unspoken national consensus to deploy the navy and air force, and sometimes even the coast guard, to the four corners of the earth, are signs of it. Despite the communal necessities that were consequences of a water-starved Great American Desert, and more lately of an urbanized culture, the product of those solitudes still resonates sharply in our behavior, and therefore in our foreign policy—a phenomenon into which DeVoto's work offers embryonic insights. In the mid-twentieth century he intuited the tension between intervention and non-intervention.

DeVoto in *The Year of Decision* spends many pages on Mormons and Indians. He describes Mormonism as "a great catch basin of evangelical doctrine. Everything ever preached by any Protestant heresy in America, always excepting celibacy, was at one time or another preached if not adopted in Mormonry." The way west for the Mormons meant prairie mosquitoes, rattlesnakes, off-and-on purchase for the wagon wheels, no fodder for the oxen, and not enough game. Every camp became a hospital. "But this was the Church of Christ. They were escaping from their oppressors, Moses had led them out of the land of Egypt, they were going to establish Zion and build up the Kingdom." Leading the Mormons westward to the Great Salt Lake was one Brigham Young, who gave his tribe "safety, wealth, and power." DeVoto calls him "the foremost American colonizer" because he delivered the Great Basin to the United States. The Mormons were "a hard, resistant folk," DeVoto goes on, who had found "a hard, resistant land. . . . Remember that the yield of a hard country is a love deeper than a fat and easy land inspires." It is in this way that the spectacular geography of the arid West and lightly soiled Rocky Mountains became iconic to the American identity (and this is to say nothing of blistering Texas, a place that developed from its first settlers—onward to its present-day inhabitants—a sense of passionate possession). The Mormons, their "crazy quilt of dogma" notwithstanding, thus become a vehicle in human form for DeVoto to define how the horizontal emptiness of the treeless West—where perspective disappeared amid shimmering distances—shaped what it still means to be an American.[17]

DeVoto writes about the Indians primarily through the literature of Francis Parkman, a Harvard graduate and Puritan Brahmin who headed west in 1846 to live among them, arriving at Fort Laramie in the Wyoming badlands in June, in a region that DeVoto labels "the desert of Isaiah." Parkman may have been stuffy and elitist, but his accounts of what he saw were firsthand and first-rate—his journal filled with Indian ways, beliefs, and traditions—and thus cannot be easily ignored. DeVoto, channeling Parkman, exclaims about the Indians, "How admirably fierce, strong, tireless, and male!" And yet they were "a neolithic people, an anachronism embedded in the eighteen-forties," as he goes on to describe the Oglala, Apache, Pawnee, Cheyenne, Comanche, and other tribes, explaining how the Plains Indians were the fiercest, because of the lack of geographical protection and boundaries inherent in their surroundings.[18] DeVoto's and Parkman's descriptions are both specific and frank, even as they unfortunately make no allowances for the sensitivities of the current era. In DeVoto's prose, there are no generic Native Americans as they sometimes exist in today's lexicon: there are instead different tribes with their very specific characteristics. Parkman actually lived among the Indians, and DeVoto, himself a westerner, was much closer in time to them and their free way of living than almost anyone alive today—thus it is important to keep his prejudices in perspective. Stegner, in *Beyond the Hundredth Meridian* (1954), probably explains these issues in a far more analytical if tragic manner: "The industrial culture was certain to eat away at the tribal culture like lye.... What destroyed the Indian was not primarily political greed, land hunger, or military power, not the white man's germs or the white man's rum. What destroyed him was the manufactured products of a culture, iron and steel, guns, needles, woolen cloth, things that once possessed could not be done without."[19]

DEVOTO'S AT TIMES CRUEL, gaudy, cinematic rendition of Manifest Destiny ultimately congeals into a tale of tragedy and redemption, between brief but riveting portraits of seemingly everyone of the era from Polk to Thoreau, to the protean southern firebrand John C. Calhoun, to the great mapper of the Rocky Mountain West John Wesley Powell, and so on. It is a history against a backdrop of "alkali, sagebrush, wind, and water" that young Americans in school today desperately need to know about, even as it will probably never be taught or appear in many of their textbooks, owing partly to the intensifying censorship of an academic clerisy.[20]

DeVoto chronicles the heroic exploits of the American troops who trekked to Mexico through the bleakest of deserts in 1846 to fight the Mexican War, a war of naked territorial expansion. He informs us about how Americans drifted into that conflict whose full implications they did not understand, believing wrongly that any war they fought had to be a righteous one. And so the young country's mood blackened amid its seventeen thousand casualties. "It was a faintness, a shrinking back while the feet moved forward in darkness, a premonition more of the lower nerves than of the brain. Something had shifted out of plumb, moved on its base,

begun to topple down. Something was ending in America, forever."
In Mexico, America had lost another measure of its innocence.
Thus does DeVoto set up the Civil War as a postscript to his story.

The Civil War, according to DeVoto, was about "Yesterday"
versus "Tomorrow": Yesterday being the South with its slavery and
plantation culture built on one crop, cotton; Tomorrow being the
industrialized North and its aversion to slavery. After quoting Lincoln on why—"Physically speaking we cannot separate"—DeVoto
goes on to explain that "Mr. Lincoln was telling his countrymen
that the achieved West had given the United States something that
no people had ever had before, an internal, domestic empire, and
he was telling them that Yesterday must not be permitted to Bal-
kanize it."[21] What Lincoln knew about the western territories from
his own experience on the Illinois prairie and travels down the
Mississippi River, DeVoto had to reteach us in the middle of the
twentieth century. It now has to be taught again in an age where
technology tricks us into thinking geography irrelevant.

THE YEAR OF DECISION constitutes DeVoto's broad-brush treatment of westward expansion and the interplay of geography and
raw human ambition that realized it. The second part of the trilogy, Across the Wide Missouri, published in 1947, is a narrower, deeper,
Proustian dive into the subject, using the Rocky Mountain fur
trade as a literary organizing principle. Here DeVoto contrasts the
prairie—God's country, Lincoln's West, with its rich soil that could
feed a continent—with the Great American Desert west of the
Missouri River, whose aridity constituted the most pivotal discon-

tinuity in young America's emerging imperial expansion. Both prairie and desert were flat and treeless, but one had water and tall grass and the other had little water and consequently short grass. One served as an organic extension of westering beyond the Appalachians; the other was a barrier that had to be overcome one way or another. Indeed, it was overcome eventually by a combination of technology, community, and governmental oversight—all of which DeVoto vigorously supported, even as he condemned the myth of frontier individualism. DeVoto never stopped being liberal.

DeVoto compares the Great American Desert, or Great Plains as they are now properly known, to "the steppes of Tartary." The object, as he intuits the minds of the pioneers in all of their fantasies, was to somehow cross Tartary and the Rockies beyond in order to reach the more congenial and fecund landscape of "fair" Oregon, which the pioneers likened to Kentucky. Accordingly, they fell in love with it, though few had sighted it, as it lay thousands of miles distant.[22]

On the prairie, just before the Great Plains, lay exotic St. Louis, which the author calls "mistress of the western waters," where the Missouri flows into the Mississippi. In 1833, just as the steamboat age was about to reach "flush times," St. Louis had a population of seven thousand. "The Indians and trappers and voyageurs who brought a barbaric color to the cobbled streets were of the West, and an old and rich aristocracy, dating back long before Mr. Jefferson's Purchase, were borne on their shoulders."[23] It was from St. Louis that the fur trappers set out across the Great Plains, helped by the Missouri, Platte, Yellowstone, and Green river systems, in order to reach present-day Wyoming and Utah on the other side of the highest ridges of the Colorado Rockies—the heart of the trade in the early and mid-nineteenth century. St. Louis was a gathering place, as full of stories and adventures as any on the planet then, a place to which to return alive and laden with pelts and to gear up once more. In the 1980s, foreign correspondents knew places such as the St. Louis of an earlier age: Peshawar and Beirut, from where they made forays into war-torn Afghanistan and Lebanon.

There were, too, the mountain men, often indistinguishable from the fur traders, who disappeared from European civilization for months at a time into the "beauty and sublimity" of places like the Tetons and Snake River valley. It is with them that the Indian trade and the fur trade coalesced, for it was with the Indians that the white men traded for furs and other trinkets. This allows DeVoto to engage in many disquisitions about such tribes as the Flatheads, Nez Perces, Crows, Delawares—friendly in differing degrees—and the "teutonic" Blackfeet, the most "Prussian" of them all:

> Their overbearing arrogance, their military pride and ceremonialism, the fastidiously sensitive brutality of their honor, the childlike fondness for goosestepping in magnificent uniforms of a stone-age mentality prolonged into the nineteenth century had an intensity hard to realize today.[24]

In tone, this reads as little different from the descriptions of African tribes as recorded by European colonialists of earlier centuries. It is racially unsympathetic and therefore tactless by contemporary standards—a blemish on DeVoto's reputation. And yet he admits that the Indians were the "first victims" of "a proliferation of a [white settlement] system of financial control which converted property, manipulated credit, and stripped the resources of the plundered province[s] to the sole end of canalizing eastward whatever wealth the West might produce."[25]

Considering the abundance of his information and descriptive prose, to say nothing of his relentless passion, DeVoto's regrettable view of Native Americans simply does not establish a reason to dismiss or forget his classics of the American West. Here, for instance, is writing that approaches that of the greatest twentieth-century British literary travelers, as he describes a caravan plodding,

> under the weight of sun, under the steel-white zenith, under the rippling canopy of brown and bitter dust. Eyes narrowed by the glare were red-rimmed with alkali. Alkali smelled too, like the vague nastiness of a chemistry laboratory, but not enough to overcome the reek of turpentine and resin from the hot sage—yet when the wind coming up from [the] Green River drove the dust momentarily away, one's lungs took in a clean, electric air. Voices were microscopic in space, cursing the cussedness of mules.[26]

This was the Great Basin in 1836. Indeed, there is a feeling when reading DeVoto that *this was how it was.* We can only know how it was through literature. And so without DeVoto's literature we cannot fully appreciate America's present situation as a vast, just-conquered continent in an increasingly smaller world.

———

THE COURSE OF EMPIRE, published in 1952, completed DeVoto's trilogy of the West. It begins with the first fevered expeditions northward from Mexico by the Spanish explorers Álvar Núñez Cabeza de Vaca and Francisco de Coronado: men who were only half aware of the significance of what they had found, for there were no cities of gold or large native populations to plunder in the temperate part of the continent, only fertile soil for which hard work was required to yield a result. This third part of the trilogy ends with Lewis and Clark sighting the Pacific, in full awareness, unlike the Spaniards, of what they had discovered. In the pages between, the geopolitics of North America are slowly realized. The original fantasy of a Pacific nation entertained in the thirteen colonies is achieved after all—along with, finally, a route to India from the Pacific.

"One of the facts which define the United States is that its national and its imperial boundaries are the same," DeVoto explains. "Another is that it is a political unit which occupies a remarkably coherent geographical unit of continental extent."[27] America's greatness, ultimately, is based on it being a nation, an empire, and a continent rolled into one. And if any one piece of imperial-inspired geography accomplished this, it was the Louisiana Purchase, which it was Lewis and Clark's task to explore. As DeVoto notes, after the 1803 deal between Jefferson and Napoleon for the territory, the plural *these United States* slowly becomes *the United States* and takes on a singular verb. The Civil War notwithstanding, the filling out of a continent would work to unite the country, north and south. Geography had ordained it.

The river system of the midwestern prairie is DeVoto's prime example of this natural unity. America has more miles of navigable inland waterways than the rest of the world combined: this was arguably the original element to its economic greatness. "On the map the rivers look like the veining of a leaf. Miami, Wabash, Illinois, Wisconsin . . . Ohio, middle Mississippi—and the continental arch through which the Missouri empties into the Mississippi." Thus, crossing the Appalachians the pioneers found themselves in a flat heartland connected everywhere by rivers "where nothing could be separated from anything else. . . . Where all cultures and all stocks and all casts of thought and all habits of emotion mingled. . . . This continuity and integration of the land . . . was a centripetal force, a unifying, nation-making force."[28] The settlement of the midwestern prairie ground up the differences of the various immigrant groups into one national culture and so provided the ballast for the leap that would be required in exploring and finally overcoming the geographical disruption of the Great American Desert and Rocky Mountains, in all their dangers and vastnesses.

THE LATE DUKE UNIVERSITY scholar Louis J. Budd wrote that "a marrow-deep part of the American character still responds to the saga of the covered wagons and makes women sue now to become tank commanders and fighter pilots." And no one, in Budd's estimation, captures that story as well as Bernard DeVoto with his "twanging, bull's-eye" prose.[29] Yet literary critics, particularly those in post-Vietnam America, have never really approved of the frontier—so removed as it is from their own urban landscapes, and with its pioneering emphasis on *doing* rather than on thinking or imagining. The frontier embodied William Carlos Williams's exhortation in his epic poem *Paterson* (1946) that there are "no ideas but in the facts."[30] This ran against the abstractions of modernism and postmodernism predominant since the early twentieth century (a reason why Williams himself is perhaps less recognized than Ezra Pound or T. S. Eliot, even though he was a better poet than the former). Thus, we come to the ultimate explanation for DeVoto being forgotten by the literati: because, in the way of Norman Rockwell's illustrations, his portraits of the West are *just there,* undeniable in their vigorous nuts-and-bolts reality, literal in their depiction, averse to any theorizing or even reflection. Of course, just as Rockwell is a limited painter (an illustrator, really), DeVoto is a limited writer. He is certainly not deep: he does not bring you to weighty, philosophical levels of thought in the way that true literature does. He was a national writer at a time when the intellectual world was moving quickly in the direction of cosmopolitanism. DeVoto may very well have been, as the leftist aesthete Dwight Macdonald once alleged, merely a "middlebrow."[31] But DeVoto was a middlebrow who had made a greater contribution to American letters and America's sense of itself than many a highbrow. Though he was obviously no intellectual on the scale of someone like Edmund Wilson, against whom he sparred, DeVoto nevertheless possessed a sensibility about America's geographical situation that is quite pertinent to our foreign policy decisions today.

———

DeVoto's worldview actually achieved full force in an early
book of his, *Mark Twain's America,* published in 1932. Twain's forma-
tive experiences—which contain the core of his great works—
occurred in the riverine, prairie heartland of the mid-nineteenth
century that would later be the backdrop for DeVoto's own *Year of
Decision.* The Mississippi was the great artery of the continent, and
life along the river in the 1840s and 1850s demonstrated "an ac-
celeration" in the development of the American character itself: a
process that Samuel Clemens (later Mark Twain) observed firsthand. "The steamboat age," writes DeVoto, which provided Clemens with his most graphic early memories, "perfectly expressed
America. Even the débris through which it passed was vital and
eloquent—the dens at Helena and Natchez and all the waterside
slums; the shanty boats with their drifting loafers; the boats of
medicine shows, daguerreotypers, minstrel troupes...thugs,
prophets, saloon keepers, whoremasters," DeVoto goes on. "The
squatters on the banks and the unbelievable folk of the bayous. It
was a cosmos."[32]

Some literary critics of the time lamented the fact that a genius
such as Twain did not have a richer, subtler fabric from which to
work—the fabric of Europe, for instance. In response, DeVoto
thunders that nothing in the world bore greater literary riches or
merit than what the young Clemens had in fact beheld: the immensity of the Mississippi. Twain, even as he depicts deception,
pettiness, cruelty, racism, and jealousy in his 1885 masterpiece, *Adventures of Huckleberry Finn,* does not convey the disenchantment with

America and its eventual tragic outcome perhaps as, say, Herman Melville does in *Moby-Dick. Huckleberry Finn,* in its telling of the dramatic journey down the Mississippi on the rising June flood of Huck and the slave Jim, speaks, in DeVoto's estimation, of continental majesty and the "shrewdness" of the American mind upon which the nation would be able to draw in the years ahead: the worst years of the mid-twentieth century, in fact. With Huck on his raft floating down the great highway of what would become the lower forty-eight states, DeVoto writes, "goes a fullness made and shaped wholly of America."[33]

The same could be said of DeVoto himself. When we think about what we must do in the world, or what we must not do, we must think about who we are and what we have been. We must think of where we as a people have come from. For the settlement of the continent concerns even the most recent modern immigrant from India or China or Mexico. It is the indispensable pathway for seeing where America stands in relation to other continents and other nations. Bernard DeVoto knew its contours as well as anyone. His work, by delineating the geographical raw material of an emerging nineteenth-century republic, is now essential in order to comprehend the America of today.

III

NOTES ON A VERTICAL LANDSCAPE

So I DEPART: INSPIRED BY MY FATHER, ORIENTED BY DEVOTO. THIS is the ultimate journey: more so than any of my journeys across Oman or Afghanistan or China, the journey I always wanted to take as a boy but could not because of family circumstances. I last crisscrossed the United States twenty years ago in the mid-1990s, as a journalist and travel writer interviewing and mini-profiling people wherever I went. Those interviews revealed to me a land in dramatic, dynamic, and cruel transition: shelled-out, hopeless inner cities; survivalists with gun-and-flag fetishes in the desert; Latin culture, both low and high, moving north; environmentalists alienated from traditional patriotism; a global civilization with accents of Asia, India, and Latin America erupting particularly in some of the eclectic cities of the Pacific Northwest. Everywhere there were people intensely focused on their own local history. The more development, the more burrowing into these usable pasts. I also saw assembly-line casinos, the social devastation of Indian reservations, and, on the other hand, places deep in the continental interior dependent on the world economy and its myriad of possibilities.

But this time I require a radically different, more cerebral experience: not that of a traveler, nor that of a journalist, but that of an analyst. A traveler and journalist constantly talks to people; what they tell him helps shape his experience and perceptions. An analyst thinks about what is not being said but what is obvious. An analyst works inside the silences. And I want silence in order to contemplate nothing less than the American continent and what its international role will and should be in the twenty-first century. This is to be a landscape meditation about America's place in the world. I want to think about this, mind you, not exactly in silence, but while hearing the voices of people at the next table in my ear. If you ask people straight out about such things as politics and foreign policy, they will often as not adopt a pose: after all, they don't know you, and they may be uncomfortable about being quoted in public. Moreover, the fact that they answer your questions does not always (or often) mean that they really and truly care about the subject you have raised. Thus, their answers do not mean that the issue at hand actually matters in their lives. And so I want to overhear what people talk about when among friends and acquaintances—I want to understand their true concerns and preoccupations—and consider that along with everything else that I observe. I may be able to think more clearly about foreign policy while on the road in America than I sometimes can at meetings and events in Washington. There are flaws in this approach, certainly, but at least it may offer a different dimension of experience than what I had the previous times crossing America.

As Walt Whitman wrote in his "Song of the Open Road" (1856), I am "done with indoor complaints, libraries, querulous criticisms." I want only to see what is out there before I reflect on America's place in the world and construct a strategy for how to deal with it.

Our place in the world, I should say. For while globalization is undeniable and identities have become richer, more complex, and cosmopolitan—mainly toward a good result—a basis in particularism is still required for national coherence. Without that coherence, an effective foreign policy, for example, is impossible. So I will say *our* and *we* whenever it suits me, even as I notice that editors, mindful of a global audience, increasingly flinch at those terms. For when people in the upper reaches of government meet to discuss fateful choices, *our* and *we* are consciously employed. Thus I must do likewise. It is still a nation across which I depart.

I DEPART IN THE SPRING OF 2015, in the quiet before the presidential primary season begins, from my home in Stockbridge, Massachusetts, where the sharp, determined lines of steeples and old houses manifest the tight certainties and revealed truths of the early settlers. In places the windy emptiness of this landscape, marked by the Housatonic River and fieldstone walls, suggests the frontier that Stockbridge once was. In the early eighteenth century, Stockbridge and other towns nearby constituted the western edge of European settlement in North America. Being on the frontier, as I've said, required doing rather than imagining: clearing land, building shelter, obtaining food supplies. Frontiers test ideologies like nothing else. There is no time for the theoretical. That, ultimately, is why America has not been friendly to communism, fascism, or other, more benign forms of utopianism. Idealized concepts have rarely taken firm root in America, and so intellectuals have had to look to Europe for inspiration. People here are too busy making money—an extension, of course, of the frontier ethos, with its emphasis on practical initiative.

Perhaps it was the extreme climate of New England and the rest of eastern North America—with its dampness, freezing cold, and oily summer heat—that led not only the Native American cultures but also the European one that replaced them to be more functional and utilitarian than those in Europe. Americans rejected every ism, and that has been to the good. Even the "European Enlightenment," Daniel J. Boorstin, the late librarian of Congress, has written, "was in fact little more than the confinement of the mind in a prison of 17th- and 18th-century design." The Enlightenment, Boorstin argues, "itself acquired much of the rigidity and authoritarianism of what it set out to combat." The Enlightenment was too scientific, rational, and deterministic. In western Massachusetts, and elsewhere along this icy, unforgiving frontier, the Enlightenment encountered reality and was ground down to an applied wisdom of "common sense" and "self-evidence."[1] In Europe an ideal could be beautiful or liberating all on its own; in frontier America it first had to show measurable results.

The Enlightenment *philosophes,* comfortable in their salons, saw the state as the proper and rational instrument of progress; on the virginal slopes of the Appalachians, the state was fine so long as it did not get in the way of development. Because the Enlightenment was an intellectual discovery, it was, inevitably, elitist; whereas an oral philosophy of common sense issued here from the bottom up. To wit, the separation of church and state in America was no *beau idéal* but a practical response to the fact that the rugged pioneer spirit of optimism and free thought begot different Protestant sects, and none of them held sway over the new political establishment. These sects competed fiercely for souls throughout New England. For one of the relatively few times in recorded history, faith became purely a matter of choice. Such free religious competition and the fervor that ensued became known as the Great Awakening. Indeed, democracy in America was the product of a specific culture's interaction with a harsh landscape.

The native inhabitants were part of that landscape. The Stockbridge Indians soothed the soul of Jonathan Edwards, the severest Calvinist of the Great Awakening, who came here in 1751 to write and to minister to them as part of an exile from the swirl of doctrinal controversy he had stirred up farther east in Northampton, Massachusetts. The Native Americans here were the first to be granted U.S. citizenship, in honor of their service as scouts in the Revolutionary War. But that is local minutiae, and the broader picture counts for more.

King Philip's War, in 1675–78, fought between Native Americans and English colonists in New England, was as brutal as any spate of European atrocities, with native and white civilians, many of them children, central to the carnage. The settlers' losses were truly awful, but the war's end saw the virtual extinction of native life in southern New England. Though Native Americans fared better in western Massachusetts, the very process of development, combined with unsavory land deals, drove them onto reservations. The horrifying fact is, as King Philip's War proved, removing the Indians was eminently practical for the settlers: the same ground-down, applied wisdom that had made some of the rarefied notions of the Enlightenment unusable for ruthless pragmatic settlers in North America also closed the door on accommodation with the native inhabitants. And here is an even more troubling reality: much or all of what America has achieved domestically and inter-nationally in the centuries since might have been impossible had its dynamic new capitalist society—which emphasized self-discipline and industry and allowed the individual to rise above the group—been diluted and altered by the mores of the native culture.

History, according to its Greek root, means merely a narrative, and a narrative that is rich and deep is often unresolvable. The American narrative is morally unresolvable because the society that saved humanity in the great conflicts of the twentieth century was also a society built on enormous crimes—slavery and the ex-tinction of the native inhabitants. (And measuring one against the other would become not less but more difficult as I traveled and considered America's role in the world.)

History, though, can also be the story of ideas—and the more useful the idea, the greater the history. America's was an anti-idea: philosophers generally know less than the masses, which, left alone to seek their own interests, often know best. Such democratic populism tempts narrow-mindedness, cruelty, and barbarism, and it cannot be successfully applied everywhere, even if Americans—the missionary zeal of the Great Awakening still within us today—believe otherwise. Nonetheless, America's democratic populism broke ground here in New England, where the necessities of frontier life overthrew Europe's established hierarchies.[2]

I HEAD SOUTH THROUGH Connecticut and New York, meeting the sea at Long Island's North Shore.

Everything about Sagamore Hill is invigorating. It starts with the briny odor of the salt marsh that announces Cold Spring Harbor, an iron blue channel leading to Long Island Sound and the Atlantic Ocean beyond. Behind the salt marsh is a patch of eastern woods that, in turn, gives out to the triumph of a rambling, wide-porched Victorian estate completed in 1886. The cavernous interior of the house is dark and prosperous with oak, walnut, and cypress paneling, made delightfully ominous by the wall-mounted heads of deer, oryx, elk, moose, and buffalo and the skins of zebra and mountain lion mixed in with the red Oriental carpets on the floors. This was the summer White House in the first decade of the twentieth century. Pure energy and manliness, of a kind much less tolerated today, emanate from these rooms: the decoration of which, right down to the vast shelves of dim hardcover bindings, Theodore Roosevelt—who famously read a book a night—truly earned.

Rarely does the spirit of a man so inhabit a house as that of

Theodore Roosevelt at Sagamore Hill. It is the spirit of both in-herited wealth and the eventuating wealth that comes with the projection of territorial power and the spiritual appropriation of foreign landscapes. Teddy Roosevelt might not have fought a great war during his eight years in the White House. But he virtually built America's first industrial-age navy, and, to a degree of perhaps no other president before or since, he specifically *imagined* the United States as a global force without equal.

Long Island Sound and Sagamore Hill demonstrate what Roo-sevelt was born into: Harvard and East Coast aristocracy. His birthright gave him a platform without which his extraordinary life would have been impossible. Yet, in order to become one of our greatest presidents he had to enter upon a hard road, which at times meant obscuring his privileges, even discarding them. The fact is, Theodore Roosevelt became New York City police com-missioner, assistant secretary of the navy, hero in the Spanish-American War, governor of New York, and ultimately president of the United States less because of Sagamore Hill and what it repre-sented than because of the North Dakota badlands and what they represented. On the Great Plains in the 1880s, as a young man recovering emotionally from the death of his first wife, Roosevelt became an American. He experienced the muscular effect of a landscape upon human beings, especially upon himself, and emerged fully formed in the process: bluff, physically brave, patri-otic to the point of jingoism, undeniably passionate, intensely driven and dynamic.

He was the first American president to comprehend fully the larger meaning of the conquest of the American West—how it presaged a foreign policy of active engagement in the outside world. But the same overbearing energy that made Roosevelt an imperialist also made him a reformer. The heat, the blizzards, the foul-mouthed and bullying cowboys, and the fierce, awe-inspiring emptiness of a lawless land that admitted no tenderness—the Dakotas separated finally this young bespectacled easterner from any vestigial links to Europe. The Dakota roughnecks, in the words of one of Roosevelt's most perceptive and elegant biographers, Edmund Morris, found him "a superior being, who, paradoxically, did not make them feel inferior." It was in the Dakota back of beyond that Roosevelt began to build his constituency.

Long Island Sound might have embodied F. Scott Fitzgerald's New World, full of pregnant possibilities, limited only by man's imagination. But it offered only a glimpse of what lay farther back in the immensities of the continent. While America had had presidents from the western prairie before, Lincoln most notably, Roosevelt, by the time he began his political climb, was both of the eastern upper class *and* the parvenu American West. America became an industrial great power between the end of the Civil War and the outbreak of the Spanish-American War in 1898. Roosevelt's very person encapsulated that transformation, which happened in the course of his own lifetime. As a British parliamentarian once observed, Theodore Roosevelt "was" America—in terms of its energy, optimism, and raw potential power.[3]

HERE IS AMERICA NOW: smoke, greasy fumes, the friction of tire rubber, the memory of terrifying refineries with their rubbery rotten-egg smells. The New Jersey Turnpike has been for much more than half a century the supreme point of reference for northeasterners, anchoring as it does New York City to Philadelphia, Baltimore, and Washington, D.C., air and rail statistics still be damned. If you take Exit 6, to the Pennsylvania Turnpike, as I did with my parents for the first time in 1960 in an Oldsmobile Ninety-Eight, the New Jersey Turnpike is part of the gateway to the West: on the other side of the Pennsylvania Turnpike lie Ohio and the prelude to the prairie. I am stretching the truth, I know. But it does all begin with the New Jersey Turnpike, just as the Simon and Garfunkel lyrics suggest. In its very connectivity with the other main arteries constituting Eisenhower's Interstate Highway System, the New Jersey Turnpike, completed in 1952, helps fortify the unity of a continent on which American global power is based. For America has been the giant of the oil and gas age, an age whose end can only now, finally, be foreseen.

The New Jersey Turnpike is central to the identity of this most crowded part of the country. Those who must travel regularly on it, or at least periodically throughout their lives, know it so well that they mark their progress from one point to another by the names of the rest stops that they have memorized: Clara Barton, Molly Pitcher, Vince Lombardi, Joyce Kilmer. (How many people know that Joyce Kilmer was a man, Alfred Joyce Kilmer, a prolific poet, literary critic, and journalist killed at the Second Battle of the Marne in 1918?)

The New Jersey Turnpike once manifested liberation: the magical conquest of distance in the new automobile age. Now it bespeaks congestion and anxiety, as people's lives are busier and tenser than ever—the traffic pileups lengthen, year by year. The American population has doubled, from 157.5 million to 320 million, in the course of the Turnpike's life. The New Jersey Turnpike was never beautiful, nor is it specifically ugly. Rather, in its very absence of scenery, it is like one long, outdoor tunnel in which all the traveler can think of is getting to the other end. It is the emblem and extension of the nightmarish commute. Because America is so vast, tempting the accelerator, the commute is long and unceasing: lifelong almost, for so much of our lives passes in a *blur*. The Turnpike is the visual expression of an American economy that has ripened, settled into a stout maturity, and, in terms of the country's transportation infrastructure, is now in decline.

I drive on and witness both transformation and the fight merely to run in place. Stretches of new paving are interspersed with spine-cracking bumps and potholes. Many of the old refineries in the Turnpike's north have given way to a massive new airport, a sports complex, and the bleakness of diseased earth and brownfields. The rest stops in 1960 were clean, quiet, and you were waited on at tables. They were uncrowded, and in the age of segregation even in the North almost everyone was white. Not only was air travel then a privilege for the upper classes, so to a lesser extent was long-distance car travel. As a child, the only time I experienced what I thought of as luxury was on the road in America. By the late 1990s, these same rest stops had become crowded, filthy, a mixture of both whites and African Americans, and offered only self-service junk food with its industrial, fried smells. Now in 2015 there is another transformation. The self-service junk food is still there, but in addition there is a delightful variety of salads, croissants, fruits, healthy cereals, and gourmet coffee. Cleaning crews are nonstop and speak not only Spanish but other exotic languages. The crowds seemingly arrive from the world over, thanks to Asian, Indian, and Latin American immigration. Television news and sports blast on separate monitors. The country has changed, and will keep changing. The quiet is gone, but so is the privilege. Like airport security installations, turnpike rest stops reveal America as the great equalizer. The world of that segregated restaurant in Virginia where my parents stopped with me as a boy is thankfully gone.

I can't help but notice that the verges of the Turnpike are filled with weeds and rubble. I think of the neat rows of poplars, forsythias, and various blooming trees planted alongside highways in China that I have seen. China is a new industrial and postindustrial society; America a much older one. China may have the initial advantage, but the vitality of a still boisterous and faction-ridden democracy, with all of its limitations on maintaining infrastructure in the face of insufficient investment, is pivotal: that may be the real test of maturity. Maintenance, especially against the odds, is a testament to belief in the future.

Across the Delaware River, the Pennsylvania Turnpike, the big monster of the Northeast, all 360 miles of it, takes over. Everywhere there are Jersey barriers, orange and white cones, and signs indicating repairs and highway widening, with work crews in action. The maintenance is unceasing.

———

WHEN MY PARENTS FIRST took me to Valley Forge in 1962 it was a state park in a somewhat wild and bucolic setting. Now it is a National Historical Park in the midst of Philadelphia's outer western suburbs, adjacent to malls, office buildings, highway noise barriers, and a towering casino complex. The state park designation had served to preserve the land on which General Washington had spent the winter of 1777–78 with his beleaguered and badly provisioned Continental Army. Here his troops survived against the elements and were molded into a unified, professional force, thanks to the help of the Prussian baron and drillmaster Friedrich Wilhelm von Steuben.

From that first visit more than half a century ago I remember the three- and six-pound field artillery pieces and the rows of Continental Army huts that had been reconstructed in the 1940s and 1950s. Now the U.S. Park Service has erected a visitors' center and changed the landscape utterly. There are multiple parking lots, trolley tours, new roads within the grounds, more historical markers and other signage: even with the cannons and huts, the park itself has acquired a very suburban feel. But to say that my parents blessed me with the memory of the original wilderness would not be accurate—it had already been transformed long before my lifetime.

For by the time Washington's army left Valley Forge, deserting its 1,500 huts and two miles of fortifications—having made it the fourth largest city in America at the time—his twelve thousand soldiers had foraged the area for miles around and burned all the firewood they could find. The Dutch elms and chestnuts that Washington and his men saw were gone long ago. Valley Forge had been reduced to a wasteland, which would eventually be made worse by the Industrial Revolution as it gained force throughout the nineteenth century, with its nearby limestone quarries and belching, filthy plants. It was the centennial of the United States in 1876, coupled with the increasing despoliation of the American landscape caused by the Industrial Revolution, that sparked the movement to preserve natural and historic sites like Valley Forge. The pristine landscape I saw as a boy with the oaks and sycamores was not the original one, but a reconstructed one, too. The more crowded and developed the country became, the more manicured and suburbanized its historic sites became as well. But the main thing to realize, aesthetics aside, is that they have been preserved with the most precious, loving attention: a mundane yet over-looked portent of a healthy, national identity.

A National Park Service ranger explained to a crowd how Baron von Steuben taught the Continental Army everything from the way of marching, to the order of battle, to the structure of units. The Prussian baron laid the basis for the noncommissioned officer corps of today's U.S. Army in Afghanistan and Iraq. We became a nation, in part, by first becoming an army. That happened here, over the winter of 1777–78, and therefore Valley Forge is a foun-dational place, central to who we are. It was why among the crowds I spotted many an Asian and Indian immigrant family, the mothers in saris quietly advising their children to listen to the rangers, especially at Washington's small headquarters, which, they were told, "was the Pentagon" of its time. America is a paradox: a blood-and-soil homeland whose values, while defended from its inception by men at arms, are neither militaristic nor based on sect or ethnicity. It has the power of blood without being of blood.

THE GPS IS MY enemy, because it steers me only onto the interstates. I ignore it and turn onto the Old Philadelphia Pike headed west. The sprawl of Philadelphia suddenly vanishes and paneled fields of cultivation arise on swells just steep enough to suggest grandeur. The names on the mailboxes are Dutch and German. The silos and farmhouses are peeling and in need of renovation, and are interspersed with tasteless ranch houses and prefabs. I see men in high-crowned straw hats, beards, and suspenders, driving and riding in horse-drawn buggies, the women wearing bonnets and occasionally riding old bicycles. Their Mennonite churches are squeezed between minimarts and gas stations and drowned by cute signs. There are molded black plastic trash bins. The quaint and funny names of the towns—White Horse, Bird-in-Hand, Intercourse—are those of the northeastern tourist bible. It all goes by in an instant, as the smells of manure and fertilizer fade and the office parks and banks of Lancaster appear. Amish country is being slowly crushed by development and globalization, even as the tourist industry fights back by the very commercialization of it. What I remember as haunting and austere as a child is now almost tacky. The American roadscape increasingly resembles that of the developing world. Everything is neither-nor—neither rural nor urban, that is—and the fusing of the two lacks any traditional aesthetic. Economic and social upheaval is rarely pretty.

I STOP IN LANCASTER to visit the James Buchanan home for the first time in fifty-three years. It has barely changed, with the guides in the same period costumes. There is a nineteenth-century patrician majesty to the interior decorating; I grasp instantly why it so affected a boy of a working-class Queens neighborhood. I think of how happy I was there with my father—how wise and learned he seemed in such moments. Now a few feet away is a modern visitors' center dedicated to the history of America's fifteenth president. No matter that he might have been our worst president—because he was of Lancaster, the wealthy of the community have invested money in this center. Americans may not be taught their history well in schools these days, or even at universities, but the preservation and commemoration of historic sites across the country, I would find, over and over again, has been undergoing a renaissance.

Lancaster and Harrisburg were always two distinct cities separated by Pennsylvania farmland. Now the suburban barracks extend deep into the farm fields, blurring the separation, and the traffic congestion rarely ceases. My Rand McNally road atlas tells the story: a splatter of dark yellow, indicating urban and suburban terrain—that of each of the two cities—almost touching, and forming along with York, Pennsylvania, a new micro city-state, on the way to eliminating the rural terrain between. But then in Harrisburg, the state capital, I cross the Susquehanna River, a grand and swollen abundance itself lost amid a forest expanse, which emanates still the possibilities of the New World.

As the Pennsylvania Turnpike goes on and on, the road construction and sight of earthmovers rarely cease, along with the ubiquitous cones and barrels. Now there are undefiled, undulating ribbons of cultivation, framed by deeply forested towering ridges: the Alleghenies. In political terms, as the experts tell us, between the liberal *blue* cities of Philadelphia and Pittsburgh there begins right here in Pennsylvania deeply conservative *red* Alabama. Outside a rest stop there is silence except for the wind, until I go inside: bright lights and blasting music even louder than at the road stops back east, as if to compensate for the relative lack of civilization. But even here in rural Pennsylvania I see Muslim women in robes and kerchiefs. Everyone is on his or her cellphone: a gathering of strangers with no interaction except at the cash registers. Society is rich, cosmopolitan, even as it is atomized by technology. The cars thin out and there are only the incessant caravans of eighteen-wheelers, the container ships of the interior continent. I encounter four tunnels through the limestone mountains. In 1960 they were impressive engineering feats, and the rest stops were unique in the world. Now in countries as disparate as Turkey, Bangladesh, and South Korea I have encountered tunnels, superhighways, and highway eateries just like those on the Pennsylvania Turnpike. The world has been catching up in the course of my lifetime. But America's principal advantage is still, as I would see, again and again, its geography: the sheer scale of it, something so easy to forget.

———

PITTSBURGH STEALS UP ON you. It isn't visible from afar, like the spread-thin, accidental skylines of other cities. Pittsburgh erupts, fully formed, an ideogram of deeply socketed urbanity as I approach the confluence of three rivers: the Monongahela and the Allegheny uniting at a sharp, triangular point to form the great Ohio, which itself serves as a backdrop for steeply forested hills girdled by rail lines. This is one of the most vital navigational nodes in North America. Because the Ohio flows into the Mississippi, which in turn flows into the Gulf of Mexico, the invention of steamboats gave Pittsburgh access to the world's shipping lanes. Here the French Fort Duquesne was replaced by the British Fort Pitt, in honor of Prime Minister William Pitt (the Elder), during the French and Indian War (1754–63). Ordained by geography like so many a European fortress town, Pittsburgh is wholly American in its smoky, industrial-age masculinity. On this dirty wet sponge of a day, I was overwhelmed by architecture from the medieval to the postmodern with the Gilded Age in between, all within the turn of a neck. The city is connected by heroically arched bridges: bridges that remind me of Hart Crane's ode "To Brooklyn Bridge," with all of the poem's prairie-spanning possibilities evoked in their designs. I saw Romanesque, Gothic, and Greek Revival façades setting up Beaux-Arts skyscrapers with Art Deco flourishes, punctuated by cruciform towers and lots of brick, aluminum, and tinted glass. There were the terra-cotta pilasters of the Pittsburgh Pirates' urban ballpark and the steel-framed Heinz Field of the Pittsburgh Steelers. Pittsburgh's late-nineteenth-century wealth was from oil, iron, coke, coal, and steel.[4] Now it is from major universities like the University of Pittsburgh and Carnegie Mellon and the science-based technologies that they help spawn. Because the downtown is enfolded in hills and rivers, it is a relatively small city center and therefore walkable. The shops and restaurants are edgy in their elegance and fashion. In a plush dining room, I overhear a Hungarian immigrant talk about her local physical therapy business and how she had arrived in America twenty years ago with fifty dollars. America's routine reality is still mythic, I think.

Of course, I could have altered my route and driven farther north and west into some of the bleakest, most devastated parts of Detroit and gotten a wholly different picture of America and its history. I did something similar in a previous book, *An Empire Wilderness* (1998), when I reported on Greater St. Louis and its racial problems in semi-apocalyptic terms. The violence in Ferguson, in St. Louis County, in 2014 and 2015 provided an echo of that experience. But America's urban wastelands are well-known, and their problems dominate sensationalist local news broadcasts on a nightly basis. In a larger sense, there are whole libraries of very necessary books about the problems and imperfections of America, and in particular the hollowing out of its middle class in recent decades. But I was determined to reflect not only on this, but also on the more mundane aspects of the American landscape that rarely make it into books and into the news and yet are central to the origins of American power. I want to look at the America that exists beyond the reductions of television cameras and reporters' questions.

The dark yellow blot on the map that is Pittsburgh has also spread greatly in recent decades, like Lancaster and Harrisburg. The growth of these cities, at first, both augmented and reflected American economic and cultural strength. But as even these cities of the interior continent (far away from the more cosmopolitan coasts) intimate, present and future phases of urban expansion will bring their inhabitants increasingly into a global civilization and less into a uniquely American one. It isn't just in Pittsburgh where I observe an eclectic edginess, but also in new areas of Lancaster, with its boutique hotels and restaurants serving small, artistically arranged portions that are influenced by Europe and Asia. Little by little, in minute and mundane ways, American identity, despite local historical preservation, is being diluted as America itself emp- ties into the wider world.

Ahh, the rise of liberal, Democratic blue America, you might say. But the story does not end there. Globalization creates its own back- lash. There are those, many millions actually, who for reasons of values, or psychological needs, or financial circumstances, or phys- ical appearance even, simply won't or cannot adapt to this new multinational cultural fusion. They feel their way of life is being endangered and fear being economically left behind in this new world of slim people on low-carb diets with stylish clothes: a world where both skin tone and sexual orientation are not singular but multiple, and celebrated for that. And because of the size and all- encompassing nature of America's continental geography, this backlash has created a vast and alternative universe all its own: of downtrodden, unpretty, unprogressive, often obese people, but there all the same.

———

WEST VIRGINIA WAS ORIGINALLY part of Virginia. But in the spring of 1861, upon the outbreak of the Civil War, representatives of its western counties met in the town of Wheeling in opposition to secession. The proximity of Ohio River traffic and the B&O (Baltimore and Ohio) Railroad, as well as the industry and manufacturing in the region, gave this far-removed part of Virginia an economic self-interest in the Union cause. Wheeling became the first capital of the "Restored Government of Virginia" prior to the granting of "West Virginia" statehood by the Union government in June 1863. Wheeling maintained a training ground for Union soldiers and a prison for traitors. Not long after, West Virginia's borders were settled in court. Because Pennsylvania already controlled the Allegheny, Monongahela, and Youghiogheny Rivers, it was decided to give the new state the east bank of the Ohio River; so on a map there is a sliver of West Virginia territory—a few miles only—thrust upward between the states of Pennsylvania and Ohio. West Virginia is one of the most oddly shaped of the fifty states, internally riven by mountains and including some of the poorest reaches of Appalachia, yet with a fierce sense of distinctiveness. And that is the genius of the American system—not only the genius of its democracy, but the genius of its separation of powers and institutions into federal, state, and local jurisdictions, thus creating sharp, geographically based identities.

Leaving Pennsylvania, I enter Wheeling as if into another country. The pitch-dark old brick buildings with occasional marble and iron bespeak the nineteenth-century Greek Revival, Victorian

Italianate, Gothic, and Neoclassical, a tribute to the Germanic settlers from the 1850s and afterward. But the city appears as if struck
by a plague. The buildings are badly in need of a face-lift. The
streets are so deserted they seem to echo—except for a few home-
less people, or those on the brink of homelessness, who had long
before fallen through the cracks. I see almost no one out in public,
anywhere, aspiring to—or even seemingly aware of—a better existence. Once or twice I spot a nice coffee shop, a nearly empty
bookstore, or a new grill that carries a vague hint of gentrification,
but it is not enough to constitute a trend. The buzz of shoppers
and the glint of new alloys and polymers I saw in Pittsburgh are
gone; so is the fashionable decor of my hotel in Lancaster. My hotel
in Wheeling, which first opened its doors in 1852 and hosted Union
generals Grant and Sherman, as well as eleven presidents, was last
renovated in the 1970s. The façade looks like a series of black eyes.
The seedy room has the odor of damp carpets and the chipped
furniture is thrown haphazardly about as if from a yard sale. I am
reminded of all the two- and three-star hotels I experienced in
Communist Eastern Europe during the Cold War. This is the best
hotel in Wheeling. I have visited many obscure cities and towns in
the Middle East and China that looked better, had better places to
stay, and where I felt more secure and comfortable. Here is where
globalization, by creating flashy and sprawling city-states, often
anchored to great universities, such as Austin, Texas, and the
Raleigh-Durham Research Triangle in North Carolina—places to
which young professionals especially are attracted—has simply
crushed smaller places like Wheeling in dying coal country. Even in

the heart of America, if a small city is not connected in some de-
monstrable fashion to other continents, it is dead.

I explore the blighted town on foot: on the main street and others there is one boarded-up storefront after another, and "For Sale"
signs everywhere. Between two empty stores I notice an adult
video shop that is open. So is a shoe repair stall. The few people I
run across are especially polite, as if no one has spoken to them in
years. The town barely has a pulse.

Then there is the riverfront: the homely, raggedy green purity of
the Ohio River valley with its iron-dark nineteenth-century house
fronts. The energetic river has already gathered the waters of the
Allegheny, Monongahela, and Youghiogheny, with many others,
such as the Muskingum and the Wabash, still to come before meeting the Mississippi. There is a new monument to the armed services in memory of all America's wars, from the Revolution to Iraq.
I buy a copy of the local paper. The headline is about hundreds
more area coal miners being laid off because of the natural gas and
fracking boom. The mills here are gone. While the town's population in 1940 was 61,000, it is now around 28,000. At night I have
a drink at the hotel bar. There are men in gas station and hunting
caps watching professional wrestling on the monitor. The volume
is turned way up. There isn't a cellphone in sight.

I DRIVE ACROSS THE BRIDGE onto the Ohio side of the river, where
I am met by dizzying piles of steep hills as dark green as seaweed. I
head south on a state road along the whispering, swirling Ohio

River. Rarely have I seen a river with such expectations of a journey, its demeanor and that of the landscape changing around each curve. This is the essence of the eastern landscape. It is vertical, built upward with tall trees and thus enclosed, claustrophobic in many places, lacking far-off vistas. The long and clarifying vision is difficult to espy. It reminds me that my journey is only beginning.

Unkempt lawns and gas stations offering lottery tickets, bait, tackle, night crawlers, "lock and load" guns, and cigarettes and chewing tobacco dominate the landscape. Limping old people, women with curlers, and what since Wheeling has become the land of obesity: an American cliché, I know, but one that it is impossible not to be shocked by, because of its repetition for what will be thousands of miles.

The middle class for a long time now has been slowly dissolving into a working class precariously on the verge of slipping into outright poverty, and also in the other direction into a smaller, upper-middle, global elite. But to actually see it, for days and weeks as I would, has made me frankly emotional on the subject. I will not see very much of a middle class in my journey at all. This thing that politicians love to talk about has already slipped from our grasp. Instead, I will encounter elegant people in designer restaurants, and many, many others whose appearance indicates they have in some important ways just given up—even as they are everywhere unfailingly polite and have not, contrary to their appearance and my first impressions of them, lost their self-respect. The populist impulses apparent in the presidential campaign following my journey of early 2015 obviously emanate from the instability of their economic situation, suggesting the anger that resides just beneath the surface of their politeness.

The landscape in Ohio is wild, shaggy, a constant reminder of the fertility of the land: an explosion of trees on every sandstone hillside, ready to overtake and smother the road; wild dogwoods, redbuds, oak, ash, birch, hickory, crab apples, sugar maples, and sycamores with their whitish leaves down by the water. What a fragile thing civilization is! Despite the clutter of mobile homes and yard sales, truck stops and repair shops, and the interminable American flags, there is an untamed quality to the Ohio River valley, vividly reflecting the frontier it once was.

Marietta, Ohio, is a rare oasis of middle-class civilization, with its domesticated riverboat-style hotel, complete with brochures and meticulous decorating. The roads have pedestrian paths and are lined with clever-looking boutiques and lively restaurants. I feel as if I have passed through a glass door from a social and economic war zone into the safety of upwardly mobile society. People have smartphones, they look presentable, and the conversations are about financial planning, new cars and appliances, and vacations in Europe and beyond. In Wheeling and in the rest of the Ohio Valley that I have seen so far, the conversations have been all local; here in Marietta, the rest of the country and the world enter into people's talk. Wheeling is dying coal country; Marietta is near natural gas fracking country. Wheeling's collapse over the years has been partially the consequence of the rise of the Highlands shopping complex in nearby Triadelphia, West Virginia, to which the commercial business in the area has migrated. The Ohio River valley, with its plants producing manganese alloys, polystyrene, and polymers, and its coal-fired power stations, is not a region in decay but one in changing, economic turbulence: the real story of the continent.

Marietta's signal advantage has always been Marietta College, a small liberal arts institution established in 1835, with among the highest academic standards in the Middle West: with students who today hail from twenty countries and stately brick buildings that are the legacy of petroleum money. Small colleges are persistent across the American continent, a legacy of its wilderness beginnings and the necessity of building a vibrant civilization upon it by way of a communal spirit—higher education spread evenly throughout the country has become a component of American power. Still, even an institution like Marietta College is now increasingly connected to the outside world, more so even than it is to other nearby towns along the river.

The way west begins in Marietta. In 1788, it was the site of the first civilian government, established by New Englanders, west of the original thirteen colonies. Thus began what in American history became known as the Northwest Territories. Marietta was a fort in Indian country, a stopping point for steamboats, showboats, and packets between Pittsburgh and the Mississippi. Along the Muskingum River, right before it meets the Ohio here in town, there is a statue of the first settlers from New England. It was executed by Gutzon Borglum, the sculptor of Mount Rushmore, in the consciously symbolic and heroic style for which he is famous: the figures seem to be thrusting themselves out of the very stone. President Franklin Delano Roosevelt came to Marietta in 1938 to dedicate the monument. On the leafy and majestic Muskingum banks there are the usual war memorials, including those to Korea and Vietnam, celebrating America's conception of a "new purpose" in world history. Even with stalemate, failure, and defeat, the conviction that America is, yes, *exceptional*—as insufferable as that may sound to many—is real and accepted without irony. Becoming reacquainted with that fact, deep in the heartland, helps stabilize your judgment about it, since it emanates from the communal experience of settling a frontier.

THE OHIO RIVER, on a spring morning in Marietta, is as wide as the universe, with a vision of heaven reflected in the water between Ohio and West Virginia. But it is not just the Ohio. Everywhere from Pennsylvania to Iowa, I will see another critical component of American power: the abundance of runs and creeks and streams feeding into the larger rivers that never cease, punctuating the sheer abundance of internal waterways on this continent. The Wabash and the Des Moines will appear as mighty as the Susquehanna and the Ohio. Then there are the Scioto in south-central Ohio, the Sangamon and Illinois Rivers that Lincoln knew so intimately, and the innumerable smaller ones that I will drive across. (I just love repeating the names: the Skunk, the English, the North and South Raccoon, and the East and West Nishnabotna in Iowa and Missouri.) The eastern half of the United States is a heavily watered, arable cradle. For someone who has lived and traveled for significant stretches of my professional life in the Greater Middle East— a region whose political problems are both directly and indirectly related to a lack of water and the virtual absence of rivers, where riverbeds are usually bone-dry—this is a revelation. You can know something abstractly and intellectually, but it is another thing to know it palpably and visually, to see the very specific geography from which history springs.

BEYOND THE EASTERN TURNPIKES the road repairs remain constant. Little is left to deteriorate, and while the country badly needs investment in infrastructure, compared to 1970, when I first crossed America, the highways have multiplied and have been enlarged. Back then, the highways had allowed for my trip in the first place, even as I was less conscious of them. They were less obtrusive, in other words. It was a time when you came upon every city suddenly, without major suburbs to ease and deflate your entry. I remember the elation I felt on every day of travel. This time I had to work harder at it.

The transportation linkages within the continent are prodigious, even as they are commonplace and thus barely worth mentioning. But that does not mean that they are not fundamental to the unity of the nation. The gas stations now get bigger as they double as food markets and rest stops, offering masses of different coffee blends without any sign of Starbucks. Despite the revolution in domestic air travel America is still a road culture, with nationalism more than globalism embedded in those whose universe is the American map and landscape. This is particularly the case with the truck drivers. But even at those road stops populated by the toughest, most grizzly crowd of customers, the stores are usually managed by women and teenage girls, to whom nobody gives a hard time. This is an intensely polite and civilized country for the most part, as much so in its own unique way as the Middle East and East Asia where I have traveled, despite its lack of high culture and so-called sophistication.

But the nightmare of uniformity—the same strip malls, fast food, and prefabricated churches along the roads and highways; the same assembly-line hotels where the room fresheners only add to the sterility and anonymity of the place; the same food marts with clipboards advertising lottery tickets, bait, and the like—only gets worse as I continue my journey. The continent is immense and the country at critical levels is culturally and materially unified, for better but often for worse. Crossing America in the early twenty-first century is a radical experience. You are like a mouse on a treadmill. Each Best Western or Holiday Inn Express is made as if out of the same machine mold, with the same juice machines and the same dispensers and Styrofoam bowls for Kellogg's cereal in the morning. You feel as if you wake up each morning in the same room, even as you are covering more than a hundred miles a day. You try different hotels, different places to eat, but it is all a matter of limited variations. The only aspect that changes is the landscape, and that happens slowly. The points of reference become more and more spread out. America is primarily about experiencing space and vastness.

The Ohio River now borders Kentucky instead of West Virginia. On the Kentucky side I encounter a group of people gathered around a gas station lunch counter to admire a newborn baby. The place has the cloying, wretched smell of fried, processed food. Nearly everyone looks poor and unhealthy. But they are dignified. They talk almost in unison about the miracle of life. They do not sound cynical or ironic about anything. Some of the old people wear service caps announcing the foreign wars in which they fought. They are all white, in jarring contrast to the eastern cities I've left behind. American flags and, again, churches are ever-present for miles around. *You have a good day,* more than one of them says to me.

This crowd and the others I encounter make me think that per-haps the most keen-eyed observer of how Americans view foreign policy—if indeed they think about it at all, except at times of tan-gible national emergency—has been the scholar Walter Russell Mead. Mead notes that while the elites in Washington and New York are either Wilsonians (who seek to promote democracy and international law), Hamiltonians (who are intellectual realists and emphasize commercial ties internationally), or Jeffersonians (who emphasize perfecting American democracy at home more than en-gaging abroad), the broad mass of the American people falls into none of these categories. They are, writes Mead, more often Jack-sonians, who believe in honor, literal faith in God, and military institutions. They may be suspicious about America's ability to perfect the world, but they will hunt you down if you insult or hurt them. America is a democracy that has a highly developed warrior ethos, making it absolutely ruthless in many of its wars. A bloody nation we have been. That is to a significant extent the result of the Scots-Irish and "redneck" traditions that have been more influen-tial in our military conflicts than other, elite traditions. The Scots-Irish immigrated to America in the eighteenth and nineteenth centuries from Ulster, settling heavily in Appalachia, and helped originate the frontier culture. Mead identifies them and their tradition with the first populist, avowedly frontier president, Andrew Jackson.

KENTUCKY IS A BORDER STATE, the northernmost limit of the South. As it happens, the book I have brought along is *The Portable Faulkner,* edited by Malcolm Cowley. Opening its pages is always like entering a dream, which I reenter every night before going to bed. William Faulkner writes about the Old South like a man possessed, as if he is under a spell and the mere transcriber of his own visions. You can't just read Faulkner: you are either addicted to him or not. With him—and more precisely with his characters—there is this overpowering, barely articulate vernacular, in which the past and present are jumbled together, oddly explaining things better than the finest intellects can. I can read only about ten pages a night. It feels like delving into a hard-to-follow dead language from antiquity: less plots than stovepipes of memory, his protagonists moving along roads measured in years rather than in miles. In a peculiar way, I have always found him the most European of American writers, not only because of the complexity of his style, with all of its psychological layers and ranks of perception, but also because the landscape he is writing about, the Deep South of old, of previous decades and centuries, has known defeat and humiliation and thus has knowingly succumbed to fate, even as its roots of hard-jawed violence are inseparable from a wilderness that has only just been cleared.

The savage eradication of the Indians as well as the totemic
crime of slavery settle like sluggish water into Faulkner's narra-
tions; you cannot evict them. The South, as it has famously been
said, has had a tragic history in a way that the rest of America has
not. Yet, in the way that his characters are so overwhelmingly
rooted in landscape, barely wrested from it actually, as if they are
still in the process of being formed, Faulkner is also among the
most American of writers. Faulkner's world is gone: it was changed
by economic development, the Interstate Highway System, and
the human agency of a federal government in Washington with its
Civil Rights and other progressive acts, even as the widespread
poverty of Faulkner's time is still there. Yet the Old South lingers
as a factor in the corrosively partisan politics of today's Washington, with the most conservative elements of the Republican Party
having as their geographical base the former states of the Confederacy, with a shadow zone of influence in the Bible Belt of the
southern Midwest. I must keep the South in mind, even as my itin-
erary bypasses it. That geography shapes this country, too. It's there,
even if I can't know its present-day reality through Faulkner.

IF A PLACE CAN be emptier and more hollow than Wheeling, West
Virginia, it is Portsmouth, Ohio. I walk the length of the main
street and barely see another soul. Almost two-thirds of the store-
fronts are vacant and the remainder have only two or three things
in the windows, which could be cleared out in five minutes. One
shop in Marietta had more items on display than in this whole
town. The most active storefront advertises "Pawns and Loans." I

am the only customer in a café-bar. The man at the counter, noticing my unease, says, "No, all the activity is not at some new mall.
This is just an old river town where there are few jobs and few
reasons to stay anymore. It's common." The population is half of
what it was in 1950. The steel mills close by have closed. There has
been migration to the cities of Cincinnati and Columbus. Un-
skilled labor has been outsourced. Big cities already hit rock bottom and have been revitalizing (Detroit even) as the young
gravitate toward them. The suburbs have spread so much that the
map of the country looks radically different from decades ago. But
I would keep noticing these once-distinguished-looking towns of
twenty thousand or so that are struggling. Perhaps they are just not
meant to be anymore, even as we revere them as traditional because of their architecture and history? Is that Darwinism fair,
though? Should we allow people to suffer and rob them of community, as the country evolves away from what they've known? It
was towns like this that were the highlights of my journey across
the country in 1970. They were the same towns my father described so nostalgically in his journeys of the 1930s.

THE HUDDLED-TOGETHER BRIDGES AND skyscrapers of Cincinnati
are another impressive eruption, much like Pittsburgh. It is in Indiana just west of here that the American landscape stretches out
and appears to yawn. The trees recede even as masses of them are
never out of sight, revealing broader fields of cultivation: corn, soybeans, and even a bit of wheat. The lazy hillsides are like cake swirls.
The farmhouses are more upscale than in Pennsylvania, West Vir-

ginia, and Ohio, with perfectly pruned foundation plantings and freshly painted white clapboard. You have entered the breadbasket. Though the fast food joints never cease, you reach a place like Columbus, Indiana, a mechanical engineering center based on outreach to the region's universities, and things change. Suddenly, the food chains become more upscale, the obesity ends, and stylish mailboxes, tony signage, *lifestyle* clinics, and a main street with new glass buildings appear. This is another middle- and upper-middleclass oasis that is a satellite of Indiana University, just forty miles away.

After another belt of oak, maple, and hickory forest like in the East—for Indiana is a geographical transition zone leading to the heart of the Midwest—a truly global civilization appears in Bloomington: miles upon miles of expensive restaurants and well-appointed people, young and old, outfitter and boutique furniture stores, you name it. Indiana University has more than 46,000 students at this campus alone, which includes schools of computing, public health, business, optometry, and environmental studies, with the engineering and agriculture departments located at the campus in Indianapolis and at Purdue, another public university in West Lafayette. The cream-colored limestone buildings with Victorian, Romanesque, and Gothic accents exude a stylistic intimacy. The Big Ten almost looks Ivy League. It reflects the educational reality of today's world in which the sciences are overtaking the liberal arts and are consequently where the money increasingly is.

When people consider the big midwestern universities, they think—because of the thought-control projected by television sports—of football teams with beefy linemen bearing Polish,

Czech, and other East European names and corn-colored hair, playing in stadiums that each seat more than 100,000. They might imagine sprawling campuses of stolid buildings, each separated from the other by hundreds of yards, in a vast and lonely part of America where space is not at a premium: thus, in the way that we all make the most tenuous associations, they imagine large student bodies in the great middle ranks of the social pecking order. They don't always think of the Big Ten as elite, in other words.

In fact, it is these schools, of which each state in the Middle West has an equivalent, much more than the Ivy League, that make the United States the power it is. Many other countries have elite schools and institutions to staff the upper reaches of their bureaucracies—France and Britain come easily to mind. What they do not have is scale—a *deep bench,* a massive complex of universities with millions of students only one or two ranks below the elite ones. What's more, it is at the bigger, only slightly lower ranked schools where much of the scientific, technological, and engineering research and training of America takes place, on which postindustrial society depends. And do not underestimate the liberal arts at these schools. In the course of my own career, I have marveled at the world-class scholars at Indiana University alone: in fields as disparate as European medieval history, Byzantine and Slavic studies, and the politics of the Indian subcontinent. Such scholars are as respected, if not more so, than those in the same fields at Yale or Harvard. The black soil of the heartland produces agricultural wealth, which is then easily transported by an arterial network of rivers (and later trains), laying the economic basis for industrial power, the emanations of which have included—and require—the

great public universities. The Big Ten is the capstone of a vast social, economic, and political process that, again, stares right at us,
even as we don't notice it.

AWAY FROM THE EAST COAST there is a reduced sense of ego and
self-absorption. The matter-of-fact, uncomplicated, and intense
politeness of the people of the midwestern states requires a height-
ened concentration on the people around you, rather than on
yourself. The politeness, because it is clearly so genuine, creates an
energy all its own. People are happy to greet you, it is as simple as
that. And it goes no further. This is not the Middle East or Africa,
where people invite travelers into their homes, or offer them tea.
Politeness is not the same as hospitality. The Middle Eastern and
African models help social stability; the midwestern model helps
efficiency and production, since it takes up less time with elaborate
ceremony, even as it eases tension and anxiety and thus allows people to focus more on work.

Whatever the media drumbeat calculated to inspire rage among
ordinary Americans at the authorities, I consistently find people
here wrapped in discussions about work, family, health, and sheer
economic survival. The media is a carapace, a noise barrier, underneath which the real drama of the nation is played out. So I am a
passionate eavesdropper on this journey: eating at the bar table
rather than in a booth, always looking to be near people in order to
hear what they are saying. People from coast to coast, I find, are
united by their worries. They speak clearly and concisely, even in a
place like Appalachia: as in the manner of song lyrics from the

1940s and 1950s, instead of the lyrics of the electronic age that constantly assault them with profanities.

They discuss church activities, movies and television shows, the horror of porn on the Internet and what should be done about it, the cost of college and the price of prescription drugs, their knee and back problems, the challenge of caring for elderly parents with Alzheimer's, debt, sports, personal finances, insurance problems, and other commonplaces. And gossip, yes, lots of good gossip about friends, even as they clearly cannot get through their lives without some literal belief in God—which occasionally they talk about, too. But this is as far as they go into abstraction. Their matter-of-fact table talk is a corollary of their uncomplicated friendliness.

As you go west, the greater and emptier distances make the atmosphere at bars and restaurants ever more intimate, as if to compensate for the loneliness outside. In western Nebraska one night, I would hear a bar-side discussion about the evolving energy situation: the eventual decline of coal and the rise of natural gas, along with the helpfulness of solar and wind power. The challenge for producers, companies, and consumers, everyone remarks, is about adapting to the federal regulations on these matters, which get more complicated and harder to predict and thus follow. All these issues have political implications, of course, but all across America I rarely hear anyone discussing politics per se, even as CNN and Fox News blare on monitors above the racks of whiskey bottles at the local bar. Hillary Clinton's emails, the Clinton Foundation and its alleged conflicts of interest, ISIS, the South China Sea, Dennis Hastert's sexual past, Jeb Bush's chances of becoming president, the Iraq War—little about any of this is ever discussed in a way that

I can overhear. An essay in the online magazine *Politico* captured the same mood that I found: on the same day, in April 2015, that the United States initialed a historic nuclear accord with Iran, the reporter could not find one person at an Indianapolis mall who knew about it or cared much.[5] I think of DeVoto's recollection of a heartland in the summer of 1940, oblivious to the world war that was about to engulf them. This is all in piercing contrast with the Berkshires, in western Massachusetts, where I live, cluttered with fine restaurants where New Yorkers who own second homes regularly discuss national and foreign issues. You may know theoretically that the Northeast Corridor is an elite media bubble, but only by crossing the country can you really know just how much of one it is, and how singular it is, compared with everywhere else.

Americans, I find more and more each day as I travel, do not want to know the details about foreign policy. It's not so different from 1940. True, we were not connected to the outside world as we are now, but neither is the global situation quite as dire as it was then. Americans don't want another 9/11, and they don't want another Iraq War. It may be no more complex than that. Their Jacksonian tradition means they expect the government to keep them safe and to hunt down and kill anyone who threatens their safety. But if you initiate violence, there had better be a good reason for it. Inside these extremes, don't bother them with the details. Despite the 24/7 media, they are not particularly interested.

I know now that tens of millions of Americans watched Donald Trump's bombast at the Republican presidential debates. But the very visceral interest in Trump is intrinsically related to the very lack of interest in politics I detected on the road. For Donald

Trump represents a sort of antipolitics: a primal scream against the political elite for not connecting with people on the ground, and for insufficiently improving their lives. People, trapped in their own worries as life becomes ever more complex, are simply alienated. And that alienation is registered in a taste for populist politicians.

You can see easily why isolationism, most memorably associated with the grand old man of the mid-twentieth-century Republican Party, Robert Taft of Ohio, constituted a venerable and respectable American tradition. It fit well with a landscape that had so much going on inside it, so that the world outside seemed never quite real. Of course, now, with an ever more urbanized and suburbanized—read globalized—America in intimate contact with other continents, isolationism loses much of its appeal, so that it is less respected. But I cannot wholly discount the absence of concern about larger issues, an absence that still coexists with an immense continent harboring so much social and economic turmoil of its own. *Leave us alone and we'll leave you alone, or else we will hunt you down wherever you are.* I induce Walter Russell Mead's Jacksonian tradition from what I see before me, even as I know that American foreign policy must be much more than that. But even if it must be much more than that, an American policymaker—no matter how idealistic, no matter how bent on improving the world and alleviating human suffering—cannot ever fail to ask himself or herself, *What can these people in the inner reaches of the country actually tolerate? What is their pain point in terms of America's actions abroad? What is their innate wisdom on military intervention, accepting that for most of them the Jacksonian tradition is their starting point?*

———

THE PATH OF THE sun demonstrates the span of the continent. As I drive west the sun sets later in the evening, even as it rises later in the morning, so that the mornings are darker and the evenings lighter. But then I cross from Indiana into Illinois, set the clock back one hour, as I am now in the Central time zone, and the process begins all over again, and again, as I cross into Mountain Daylight Time in western Nebraska and into Pacific Daylight Time in Nevada. To fly to California and set your clock back three hours is not to know the ground you have covered, because you haven't seen all the different mornings and evenings along the way.

A few miles into Illinois there is another gradation: the prairie truly begins. The earth has flattened out entirely. The tight packs of trees have receded to the edges of vision. There are miles of ribboned ground bearing corn and soybeans, punctuated by wide, circular metal silos. The native grasses and black earth alleviate the loneliness of the landscape, reminding you just how wealthy it is. Because this production and fecundity will go on for hundreds and hundreds of miles, both north and south and east and west, it constitutes the basis of continental wealth that, in turn, permits an approach to the world so ambitious—marked as it is every few decades by an epic, bloody disaster—that the human and material costs are easily absorbed by the very wealth and sheer size of the land that began it in the first place. It is these Illinois cornfields that ultimately allow elites in Washington to contemplate *action,* even as others may suffer or be sustained by the consequences.

A scene repeated over and over before my eyes: a Union Pacific freight train, stretching seemingly over the curvature of the horizon, pulling up with a groaning roar to a complex of corn or soybean silos to have its cars loaded. Such expressions of national power have not changed much in decades, but few in actual positions of power actually see or are aware of them anymore. The sight makes me humble. I know that it is the immensity of the continent that required the development of more powerful and efficient locomotives than in other parts of the world, something which, in turn, enabled the development of long-distance engines for our warships, so that the strength of our navy is directly related to the size of the dry-land continent and the rail lines spanning it.

The sight makes many midwesterners humble, too, a reason why those brought up on the prairie and Great Plains tend toward caution in foreign policy decision making. They intuit that just as the vagaries of the weather can destroy crops, other things over which we have no control can interfere with grand plans made in Washington.

Springfield, Illinois, the state capital, looks as exposed to the wind and prairie as it did in Lincoln's day. The sound of the freight trains is everywhere in the middle of the city. You see the blight of boarded-up store windows a hundred yards from the state capitol building. There are insufficient trees, and the wide gridwork of boxy concrete buildings—as though from the brutalistic 1970s— often looks indistinguishable from the parking garages. The gridwork of streets in Lincoln's day was *of* the prairie, with all of its futuristic possibilities and the grinding down of human differences. But today's Springfield looks less a place of possibilities than of being passed over by Chicago and other, more vibrant midwestern state capitals. Indeed, Chicago seems to have literally sucked the air out of Springfield: another case of America becoming a network of massive city-states more intimately interconnected with other continents than with their own hinterlands. It is in the merging with the rest of the world and global civilization that the forces of division come to the fore at home. Springfield: another small city that should inspire but doesn't.

Lincoln was *of* Springfield more than of any other place. So there is something to be learned here.

A STEADY STREAM OF visitors file into Lincoln's two-story house all day long. (A point of comparison: I was one of only three visitors at Buchanan's far more impressive mansion during an entire morning.) It was in this house on Eighth and Jackson Streets that Lincoln lived between 1844 and 1861, where he fulfilled the American dream of rising from the humblest beginnings to become a proper member of the bourgeoisie. In 1856, when he was a forty-seven-year-old lawyer, the Lincolns had accumulated enough money to renovate and enlarge their cottage in Greek Revival style, with a touch of Victorian. Lincoln had risen to this pinnacle through migration, self-education, and hard work. His whole life experience system breathed and was suffused with democracy, egalitarianism, and economic freedom—all the possibilities inherent in the frontier. Thus, he championed the building and improvement of railroads and canals as a means to incorporate that frontier into the nation. Lincoln was a man of the West as it was then conceived: the first president to have been born beyond the Appalachians, who had served in the Black Hawk War of 1832, who had been a surveyor on the prairie, and who had taken a flatboat down the Mississippi to New Orleans. He knew intimately what was at stake in the debate about whether or not to extend slavery to the western territories.

Lincoln's house is comfortable, almost prosperous, but without any ostentation or grandiosity. It is just *so* middle class, and that is why it is touching. Whereas Buchanan was wealthy at the time he became president, Lincoln was in the upper middle. Whatever the other differences between the two men, that is a crucial distinction. Buchanan's home displays the lithographs he owned of Queen Victoria and Prince Albert, people whom he had met in the flesh on quite a number of occasions as the chief United States minister in London. The prosperity in Lincoln's home is evinced mainly in the separate bedrooms he and his wife Mary Todd Lincoln were able to occupy, and the wood-fired cooking stove in their kitchen: a kitchen almost as large as the log cabin in which he was born. Buchanan was a man of the world surrounded by crystal and gold leaf and a Boston-made Chickering grand piano; here in Springfield is the tooled furniture and the fashionable wallpaper of a successful prairie lawyer.

In Lincoln's upstairs bedroom, adjacent to his wife's, is the small pigeonhole desk where he managed some of his correspondence in the months after he was elected president and before he was inaugurated, when the very country he was about to lead was falling apart. The material humbleness of the setting and the partial view of the prairie afforded from his desk while he contemplated the fate of the nation does, in fact, bring a lump to your throat. Buchanan's house is historically noteworthy; Lincoln's is a shrine. In Buchanan's house you are guided by a man in period costume who accepts tips; in Lincoln's by a National Park Service ranger, who notes that here in this house is the real Lincoln, more so than the official one you encounter at the Lincoln Memorial in Washington.

Lincoln's journey—from the Kentucky wilderness to this comfortable house near what was then the western edge of settlement— gave him a better understanding of just what was at stake in the Rebellion than Buchanan's journey had. Lincoln was a man of the western frontier; Buchanan, whose life was centered in Lancaster, Pennsylvania, was not. But by uniting the Union, ending the North-South divide, and turning America on the path toward becoming an industrialized, east-west-oriented middle-class machine, Lincoln rendered Buchanan the last of the so-called frontier presidents ever to govern America. Geography does not determine individual character, but it does matter.

Lincoln looked out over the prairie and intuited the entire globe. But someone who unites us in this era cannot be a Lincoln, since it is no longer about one political tendency in America vanquishing the other. It is about the globalized half of the population respecting and gaining sustenance (and grounding) from the nationalistic half, more rooted as this nationalistic half is in geography. For global culture has a fatal weakness. Uprooted from terrain, there is less to fight for, since the homeland means less than it used to. And by unmooring people from geographically rooted traditions, global culture makes them more susceptible to fashions and fads and eventually even to ideologies. This is what makes geopolitics that much more vicious and abstract: a sheer battle of pride and communal identity fought out over a battleground where stable, conservative tradition anchored in landscape has been, or is being, lost.

IT IS IN ITS unrelenting sameness that the midwestern landscape achieves its power. In the pounding darkness of spring thunderstorms, the gas stations and general stores are filled with light, warm conversation about the weather and its effect on the crops, communicated with camera-sharp friendliness. The sustaining rhythms of country music are everywhere, in the lavatories even. On U.S. Route 67 in McDonough County, Illinois, the heartland achieves an iconic synthesis: a black-soiled seascape of agricultural riches that Spanish explorers traveling north from Mexico like Coronado could not appreciate. These riches would require toil to bring them forth. The streams and crecks multiply. I cross the Mississippi at Hamilton, Illinois, into Keokuk, Iowa, dip into Missouri, then cross the Des Moines River back into Iowa. The eastern forest returns, then recedes, then returns once more as the flat prairie becomes a gentle, windswept sea of electric green hills populated here and there with black cattle. Because of the very size of the prairie, it has endless topographical variations.

And the historical markers never cease. Every locale is proud of its history. The more global America becomes, the more people are digging into their roots as to what role this or that place played in the settlement of the continent and the expansion of democracy. Military history—that is, the erection of forts on the prairie, plains, and mountains in order to manage Indian affairs in the nineteenth century—is paramount in importance to the people here, followed by the activities of settlers, the various steps toward equality of women and African Americans, the establishment of labor unions, and so on. There is no better, more easily accessible history for the general public than these markers and the talks given by National Park Service rangers. It is accurate, insightful, and, most crucially, balanced: immune to academic fads, yet aware of pathbreaking works of scholarship.

Meanwhile, the tale of the two Americas goes on: the industrial smell of greasy fast food and the tingle on the tongue of oaky Chardonnay in an upscale Des Moines restaurant. Des Moines, Iowa's capital, is full of flashy, stylish prosperity in both the food and the glinting architecture: the gift of an insurance industry that does not rely on state government. There is no Chicago in Iowa to diminish Des Moines. I feel a universe removed from the sleepy shabbiness of Springfield.

THE MISSOURI RIVER IS lost almost on account of the construction on both sides: in Council Bluffs, Iowa, and in Omaha, Nebraska. These cities are frightening in their gigantism. Every ramp, every highway lane, every parking lot, every mall, and the spaces between the malls and between the parking lots, and the spaces between the tables at the sprawling restaurants inside the malls—they are all on a scale of bigness that is alienating and thus intensifies loneliness. But none of it is grandiose, or deliberately imposing, or intended to intimidate and crush the individual and his spirit as Communist

Cold War architecture did, with its heavy reliance on stone and concrete. No, this architecture in Council Bluffs and Omaha, this whole deeply embedded psychology of the use of space, simply conveys that there is a lot of it. There is no need to make things smaller. That is the American condition, a source of its optimism and its unfriendliness to elites and aristocracies of all kinds, which require constraints on space in order to increase the value of their land—which then affords them their social position. This was a crucial difference between the Old World and the New. Virtually unlimited space is the essence of the frontier mentality. The American West is immanent in Omaha.

Humanity requires aesthetics, which in turn require a sense of limits and of proportion. This is why too much space is dangerous. Too much space can lead to delusions, to which America periodically falls victim. For the ultimate cause of American aggression—its belief in its own missionary values—rests on its conquest of space. But as space becomes increasingly constrained by the spread of cities and suburbs and the revitalization of downtowns, and as increasing pressure on water resources enforces limits to growth—stopping further expansion into the desert—America will have to moderate its instincts and goals if it is to continue to prosper, especially as a chaotic and unstable world moves closer.

In 1893, historian Frederick Jackson Turner famously proclaimed the end of the frontier, and thus the end of a particularly dynamic strain in American culture. But by the looks of Omaha, the frontier has not yet entirely closed. The continent is so big that there is still room to grow inside it. Moreover, the frontier was with us long enough to remain a deeply embedded national character trait, albeit increasingly faint and subtler. Just look at our foreign policy and the expansion of America's international reach since Turner's day.

The world itself has now become America's frontier. And that has been both a blessing and a scourge. Omaha's spatial arrangement offers a disturbing, almost subconscious explanation for America's imperial ambition.

NOTES ON A HORIZONTAL LANDSCAPE

THE HOUSES AND THE STRIP MALL LOOK LIKE STAGE PROPS THROWN up in the night. I hold my eyes tightly shut and the leafy suburban plots of North Omaha disappear. I imagine before me a pivot point in American history. It started at this place, one of the last outposts of the prairie before reaching the even lonelier Great Plains. For here, on this spot, was located Winter Quarters. In 1847, in the third year of James K. Polk's presidency, 148 Mormon pioneers began their trek from here to the Great Basin in Utah, to the Salt Lake Valley as it would turn out. This was before the coming of the railroad, and the hardships these pioneers bore are barely conceivable. The trek, in Wallace Stegner's words, was a "rite of passage, the final, devoted, enduring act that brought" the Mormons into the Kingdom of God, and into Zion. There is a "literalness" to Mormon belief that secularists simply cannot know, let alone imagine. For the Holy Land awaited them not in the Middle East, but in the American West. Divine intervention cleared the path for them. Rivers froze to support their wagons, quail dropped out of the sky to the starving pioneers like manna to the Israelites. These miracles came after the drumroll of massacres, nighttime raids, murders, lawsuits, and other persecutions against the Mormons in Missouri and Illinois that they were escaping from. Did not the Missouri governor on October 27, 1838, issue orders to his militia that the Mormons had to be "exterminated or driven from the state"?[1]

Some of the persecutors were right, though, in a way. For the nub of Mormonism was that it was highly regimented and antithetical to the brawling and boisterous democracy, with its emphasis on individualism, that frontier America was being built on. In truth, the Mormons, especially in their more extreme breakaway sects and other offshoots, have themselves often been full of violence and perversion: brooking no dissent, drawn to crackpot visions, to occasional militarism and atrocity even. I will not romanticize them, and neither did frontier America. President James Buchanan sent the U.S. Army to Utah in 1857 to subdue them. As Stegner explains in *The Gathering of Zion,* "Instead of celebrating the free individual," Mormonism "celebrated the obedient group.... What they went to build in the Great Basin was not a state, not a republic, but a Kingdom." It was "hierarchic, theocratic, patriarchal."

Yet, as a people they did constitute a westering movement, and never before or after in the history of Manifest Destiny was there a group of pioneers so disciplined, organized, and systematic, so communal, so group focused, and, therefore, after a fashion, so seemingly un-American. It may have taken such a communal strategy of severe restraint to open up the most hostile, waterless reaches of the American continent. It might even be argued that the Great Basin could *only* have been settled by Mormons. In their "hegira" to the Great Salt Lake, the Mormons would build roads, bridges, and communities along the way. The major highways and rail lines of today in Nebraska and nearby states began as the Mormon Trail. In fact, a third of the travel to California and Oregon by 1849 was along the Mormon Trail. This was about working within limits in order to overcome limits; it was about the triumph of the group over that of the individual.

At Winter Quarters in North Omaha, the Mormons left the settled United States and entered Indian terrain. They prayed after the fires went out and they slipped into their blankets, protected, as Stegner writes, only by their own guards and passwords. On June 27, 1847, they would trek over Wyoming's South Pass into the land of "sanctuary."[2] In their minds they were separating themselves from the Gentiles; in fact they were expanding the American Empire, and individual freedom had little to do with it.

The knife-edged, blinding whiteness of the Mormon temple in North Omaha, erected in 2001 to commemorate Winter Quarters, appears to emanate an extreme cleanliness of behavior and belief, something different from purity: something that reaches a point where religion meets ideology. A few weeks hence I will come upon the Mormon temple in Salt Lake City, with its nine-foot-thick granite walls, graced by the Mormon Tabernacle, Assembly Hall, Conference Center, history museum, two libraries, two visitors' centers, and monumental administration buildings—all of it standing amid manically tended gardens where Mormons smile and wish every visitor a good day. There is the aura of fabulous wealth, the product of a driven, corporate-style cult. It is absolutely American in the darkest way.

You can't help but think of the fanaticism inherent in the conquest of the West. Despite all of the optimism and heroism that a traditional view of Manifest Destiny connotes, we must also register the unspeakable bloodshed, the mass eradication of a native culture. An intensity of conviction like this can have its dark side. The Mormons were central to this imperial venture, even if the U.S. Army did much of the killing and forcible resettlement of the Indians. Yet the world today, without the United States as it exists from sea to sea—having conquered the West—is impossible to imagine. I am not justifying that, but I am once again pointing out the moral contradiction. The Mormons helped make America what it is, far out of proportion to their numbers. And yet now they are being contained. In Salt Lake City, the Mormon temple, which used to dominate the skyline, is diminished by nearby high-rise hotels and glitzy office buildings, with a shopping plaza that features a giant Nordstrom across the street from Temple Square. A bit farther afield in Salt Lake City are breweries with elaborate beer and wine lists where the clientele is young, thin, dressed as in New York or any European city, many of them working in the local software industry. The city founded by the Mormon leader Brigham Young in 1847 is now part of a global cosmopolitan network, with all of its so-called sin. The America that I am seeing on this journey is in the midst of its final transformation—into a universal civilization. Local distinctiveness is slowly dissolving, making it even more important to hold tight to the truths of its past and its landscape.

WEST OF LINCOLN, THE STATE CAPITAL, the slab on which Nebraska lies gradually and noticeably begins to tilt upward. The fields get vaster and the air thinner. There is a rumor of liberation. Something has happened. Wheat starts to crowd out the corn and soybeans. The first of the giant center pivots for irrigation appears, as the groundwater begins to dry up and the waterways suddenly are reduced to the occasional creek. The speed limit on the interstate rises to seventy-five miles per hour, and the road is ruler straight. I-80 is on the 150-year-old freight and mule route to the Mormon, Indian, and gold rush territories. I am in the Central Platte Valley.

Just north of the Platte River was the Mormon Trail; just south of it the Oregon Trail and the Pony Express route. The transcontinental railroad passed along here, as does the Union Pacific today. Passenger cars fade away and caravans of eighteen-wheelers take over: these are longer eighteen-wheelers than in the East, with wider wheelbases and bigger cabs and cargo vans, hauling beef and grain as they often do, with two drivers alternating use of the bunk in the cab. I have never seen such trucks. For now you are entering the real West, where the dense arterial networks of roads, waterways, and population nodes rapidly disappear and the remaining roads and rivers become vital umbilical cords connecting the East to the heavily peopled Pacific coast. Iowa, with its masses of trees, black soil, and lively green shades, indicating the touch of the human hand—along with the curves and dips in the road—is almost beyond recall. The vertical landscape has ended and the horizontal one takes over, enlarging the sky and bringing the clouds closer to the earth.

The eighteen-wheelers mesmerize me. I remember my father's fatigue from driving every night, all night. It was certainly a sacrifice for him to take us on those long road trips, which involved only more driving, on his vacations and days off.

The wind has picked up and remains steady. With few obvious landscape features, the gas station signs jump out at you like bulging, bloodshot eyes. I cross the hundredth meridian of longitude at Cozad, Nebraska. Every stretch of the highway is dedicated to the armed forces. Nearly every historical marker is about army forts built to secure the rail, telegraph, and stagecoach lines against the Indians. One marker, which I would read a bit later on, tells the familiar story of Narcissa Whitman, "trail-blazer and martyred missionary," who followed the north side of the Platte in 1836 on horseback, "becoming the first white woman to cross the American continent," and who, along with her husband, Marcus, was "massacred by Cayuse Indians" at their Protestant mission in 1847 in Walla Walla, Washington. (The Indians there were justifiably enraged at the whites for spreading measles to them.) It pains me to read these markers with their honest, nuts-and-bolts sentences in plain English and their succinctly heroic, inspiring stories. This is an older history being taught here, not the one often taught in schools and universities now, in which the story of the West is reduced to atrocity and little more. It is true that historical research is necessary to defeat jingoistic nationalism. The more history we know, the more complex the story of our past becomes and the more realistic we can be about it. But without some kind of usable past, there is no possibility of affecting geopolitics for the good. How do we know where to go if we can't draw upon some inspiration from the past? There is too much destruction coming out of the academy, not enough inspiration. We require a proper balance.

THERE IS ANOTHER SACRED BOOK I carry with me, *The Great Plains* by Walter Prescott Webb, published in 1931, eleven years before DeVoto's own masterpiece, *The Year of Decision: 1846,* a book inspired in part by Webb's earlier one. Webb, a Texan all his life, had one subject: the Great Plains as the key to unlocking the mystery of everything America was and was to become. "The distinguishing climatic characteristic of the Great Plains environment . . . is a deficiency in the most essential climatic element—water." This deficiency, Webb goes on, conditions not only plant and animal life but human life, and the institutions of men, too. Therefore, the key dividing line of American geography is the hundredth meridian of longitude, running through the heart of North Dakota, South Dakota, Nebraska, Kansas, Oklahoma, and Texas. To the west of this invisible line, in the midst of a flat and monotonous landscape, all the way to the Pacific slope, there is only an average of twenty inches of annual rainfall. The arid West begins at this demarcation. Here is where the tall grass gives way to the short grass of poorer soils. East of this line, all the way to the Atlantic, the landscape is heavily timbered; west of this line the land is mainly treeless, with some obvious exceptions like the Pacific Northwest. A vertical landscape with closed-in vistas thus gives way to a vast and horizontal one. On the Great Plains winds of extreme uniformity and velocity are as strong as at the seashore. Webb then amasses detail upon detail on the types of Plains wind, such as the chinook, the norther, and the blizzard; this is a work of geography that, like DeVoto's books, explains American destiny.[3]

The Great Plains were suited to the buffalo that grazed on the short grass, individual herds of which once numbered in the millions before the arrival of European civilization. Indian life depended on the buffalo, supplying "life, food, raiment, and shelter" to them. The Great Plains made the Indians who lived on them nomadic and nonagricultural, as well as the doughtiest holdouts against European civilization. No Indians adapted as well to horse culture, introduced in the early eighteenth century, as did those of the Great Plains, again on account of geography. The Plains Indians—the Comanche, Cheyenne, Sioux, and so on—were, like the lack of timber and water, a critical element in the barrier against European settlement.[4]

Reading Webb, it becomes clear that the history of the United States hinges on the history of the pioneers adapting to the Great Plains, or "Great American Desert" as they first conceived of it. Indeed, America's east-to-west geographical orientation, as generations of citizens have come to know it, is the conceptual and cartographic result of that successful struggle. The heroism of the Oregon Trail lay not in settling the Oregon Territory—which in many parts constituted a hospitably well-watered, timbered terrain similar to the Eastern Seaboard—but in actually getting to Oregon in the first place.

Webb advances the argument that the Great Plains stopped slavery in its tracks, predetermining the defeat of the Confederacy. As Webb explains it, "The Civil War was a conflict between sections whose differences were primarily economic." The southern system was based on "the plantation, with staple crops and slave labor." The northern system was based on "small farms, free labor, and a rising industrialism." By the end of the War of 1812, both systems were well established and the rivalry between them would be fully recognized before another two decades had passed. As long as both systems could advance westward at an equal rate, the balance was maintained and the rivalry frozen at a stalemate. But while the Great Plains were a barrier for pioneers in general, "the barrier was greater for the South than for the North." The northern system could adapt to aridity, however difficult it was; the southern cotton culture could not. Thus was slavery doomed.[5]

The Great Plains, Webb writes—particularly the southern Great Plains centered on Texas and Oklahoma—also invented the cowboy tradition, by providing the perfect natural environment for men on horseback to manage large herds of cattle over substantial distances. Ranching culture, as we know it, complete with horse, lariat, and six-shooter, emerged out of an arid and treeless landscape. And because aridity could support only a sparse population on a vast panel of semidesert, with great distances between human beings, men were "thrown upon their own resources." Self-reliance became an essential and fundamental attitude for the inhabitants of the frontier West. "The Western man of the old days had little choice but to be courageous," Webb explains.[6] Yes, courage, too, was fated by geography. The geography itself, so empty and frightening, encouraged a degree of risk taking—a fundamental aspect of the American personality.

The Great Plains shocked and changed the Anglo-European personality like nothing else had, providing it with a perspective on the natural world that it had never before encountered on either side of the Atlantic. Both in Europe and in the eastern states, as well as on the prairie (though to a lesser extent), geography was benign, with rivers and ports and a sense of protection that encouraged the development of high culture. But it is in the treeless horizontality of the Great American Desert that the West first came to be seen as spectacular, treacherous, and romantic. America as we know it, in a way, was born with this new perspective. It was a landscape that gave way to loneliness, awe, elation, and depression. One can grasp the depth of the change wrought upon men's souls simply by looking at a railway map of the United States in 1890. Everywhere east of the ninety-eighth or hundredth meridian (take your pick) the map is almost black with rail lines; west of that meridian, where rainfall suddenly decreases, rail lines just stop and are few and far between. The United States nearing the turn of the twentieth century is bifurcated between a darkened East and a lightened West.

Listen to Webb:

> The salient truth, the essential truth, is that the West cannot be understood as a mere extension of things Eastern.

Though "the roots of the present lie deep in the past," it does not follow that the fruits of the present are the same or that the fruits of the West are identical with those of the East. Such a formula would destroy the variable quality in history and make of it an exact science. In history the differences are more important than the similarities. When one makes a comparative study of the sections, the dominant truth which emerges is expressed in the word *contrast*.[7]

SIX A.M. BREAKFAST. The smell of bacon frying. The various guests of the motel, strangers all, greet one another with an emotion bordering on elation. The early morning aromas mean it is a new day and everything is expected. By 6:30, the U-Hauls, trailers, and SUVs are starting up in the parking lot adjacent to the gargantuan gas station and the interstate. Americans are most themselves and most likable when on the road. We are a restless nation. Adventurism, for better and for worse, is the bedfellow of optimism.

A sense of accomplishment builds within me: not the accomplishment of professional achievement, but something more sustaining and powerful; that of crossing great distances. For the first time since I left home three weeks ago, the goal of the Pacific does not seem far-fetched. An hour of driving brings me into the Mountain time zone. A historical marker indicates that hundreds of thousands of immigrants and others traveled west along this same route beginning in 1841. From here forward, the monuments are the roads and the passes themselves: little has been built compared to in the East. Chimney Rock, rising three hundred feet off the val-

ley floor and visible from miles away, is a sandstone cap topping a
peak of clay, more sandstone, and volcanic ash. It looks like an in-
verted funnel. This geological phenomenon is revered here as a patriotic symbol because it served as a meeting point for pioneers
along the Oregon, California, and Mormon Trails. In a jet age of
global travel, it may be hard to comprehend the power that this
monument held over the nineteenth-century immigrants heading
west, having covered 450 miles since Council Bluffs, Iowa, freezing
and sweating in creaking, bone-cracking wagons. At Valley Forge,
the landscape has been transformed since the late eighteenth century; here not. Here you get a sense of the blood-and-soil American nation with all of its cruelty.

The pioneers brought measles and cholera to the Lakota Sioux
and Cheyenne, who, nevertheless, only turned against the immigrants after the trickle of white settlers became a flood. The native
culture was one with the environment. It worked. It remains a
haunting, eerie absence, along with that of the millions of buffalo
on these high plains, particularly if you stand still, look at the emptiness, and concentrate for a few moments. The great crime is like
a stone caught in your throat. As much as you try to swallow it, by
pointing to all the good that the advanced industrial culture that
replaced the native one has wrought, you can't quite do it. Yet you
still must breathe. The only answer to the crime committed here is
for the United States to use the resulting power that has come with
the conquest of a continent in order to continue to do good in the
world. Whereas the East is heavily peopled and congested with
roads and waterways, the water-starved West is largely empty, with
relatively few pathways. Conquering it was an undeniable imperial

venture, as DeVoto in his writings ably demonstrates. And even the most enlightened empires are cruel beyond measure.

I am now on U.S. Highway 26 heading west along the North Platte River in Nebraska. The vehicles and habitations have virtually disappeared and the silence is deafening, except for the piercing sounds of finches and meadowlarks, as the plateau heaves upward in sculptural swells. There are wind- and rain-chiseled buttes and mounds towering above the high plateau of short grasses. A shallow ravine in the wilderness marks the wagon ruts of the Oregon Trail. Still not a hint of political conversation whenever I stop at the stores and gas stations, though I know Jeb Bush is being racked in the media for misstatements about the Iraq War. People at the counter of a general store are talking about a "shit tree," the Russian olive, and all the damage it is causing along the banks of the North Platte, where the cottonwoods and eastern red cedars are native. The Union Pacific freight trains are constant, one after the other, running in the opposite direction from me, transporting coal from Wyoming and elsewhere to the East. You read all the time about wind and solar power. And I will see some wind and solar farms farther west. But coal dominates the traveler's-eye view. We remain still, for a bit longer, in the fossil fuel age, the age of American dominance.

Yet the signs of embryonic economic and social division don't stop, even in the emptiness. Even in the northwest corner of Nebraska there are one or two restaurants serving Greek salads with small, exquisitely arranged portions and wine lists, where people sit alone or in pairs, silent with their smartphones: increasingly, that is *home* for them, a virtual world where they channel all their worries and fears, making the places where they actually sleep at night little by little more unreal. Then there is the rest: not even the chain restaurants, but a level below them, serving industrialized fat and frequented by a homogenized culture of working people with unfailing politeness who talk about cattle and problems with kids and financial challenges. So many of the residences I see in these towns are fixed-in-place mobile home units. There is an element of transience here (and not the virtual kind associated with the smartphone set) where people pay in cash and where pennies still matter, even as the unoccupied and awe-inspiring terrain makes you crave intimacy and permanence.

THERE IS A THIRD SACRED BOOK with which I travel, one that is an heir of sorts to the others. This book, Wallace Stegner's *Beyond the Hundredth Meridian,* was published in 1953: it is dedicated to DeVoto and is partly inspired by Webb. I believe that the basis of American power, and what America can do with it, was established by these three men in the middle decades of the twentieth century, even if that is not what they set out to do. They were merely studying geography in the full-bodied nineteenth-century sense of the word— whereby geography is a starting point for the study of history and culture—which is usually more illuminating than twentieth- century political science methodologies. Their books form a canon without which America's place in the globe and in geopolitics is harder to fathom.

The late Wallace Stegner is known to many as a formidable novelist, but I believe this book to be his most important because it fully establishes his reputation as an expert on the West, and thus as a man who understands what made this country great in a more profound way than do East Coast elites. On the third page he writes that "throughout the vast concave bowl of the continental interior was illustrated the unifying effect of geography, for here where everything ran toward the center instead of being dispersed and divided by central mountains, the people could never be divided into a hundred tribes and nations as in Europe, but must be one."[8] Yes, here he clarifies further what DeVoto had observed in *The Course of Empire* (published a year earlier in 1952): that geography simply *worked* in temperate-zone North America in a way it just did not in Europe. It worked primarily because of a flat heartland united by a complex river system that flowed generally in a unifying, diagonal direction—not, for example, like the great rivers of Russia that flow north-south at forbidding right angles to that sprawling land, and thus weaken further central control across the Eurasian longitudes. So much of our relative strength stems from natural formations that were carved from the earth eons ago.

Stegner thus establishes what Lincoln felt in his bones as a man of the prairie: that is, the essential geographical unity of the continent upon which a political unity must be built. Stegner then spends the rest of the book on the implications of that geographical unity on the arid western half of the United States. He immediately contrasts two visions. The first, by William Gilpin, an old friend of Andrew Jackson's, is that of a continental cornucopia upon which there were no limits to growth and consequent geopolitical power. The second was that of Major John Wesley Powell— soldier, explorer, and geographer of the West—whose realism was based on observable facts, and who therefore stipulated that immense stretches of the western United States were water starved, meaning that development had to be tightly regulated. In other words, even though geography had granted the American people political unity, that did not mean there were no limits to what they could do and achieve. American geography told a story of narrow constraints as well as one of unending horizons.

Stegner's book is about proving "Wes" Powell's vision correct, and so Powell becomes the hero of the narrative. Powell *was* westering mid-nineteenth-century America personified, with a migratory and hardscrabble boyhood that took him in stages from New York to Ohio to Wisconsin to Illinois, and up and down the Ohio, Mississippi, and Missouri Rivers. In 1862 during the Battle of Shiloh, while fighting for the Union in the Civil War, he lost an arm above the elbow. Stegner writes that the handicap "affected Powell's life as much as a stone fallen into a swift stream affects the course of the river. With a velocity like his, he simply foamed over it." Powell's great lifetime feat, which more than any event gave him a philosophical orientation on the dangers and limitations of the mountain West, was his 1869 expedition through the Green and Colorado Rivers, from present-day Wyoming, down through the entire length of Utah, to Arizona: the least-explored large tract of the West at that point in time. The precise courses of these rivers were not yet known, and the map in general in the Great Basin was full of "blankness."[9]

The rapids were frightful and the portages backbreaking against a monumental landscape of mesas, broken rock, vermilion canyons, and "bizarre forms of desert erosion." Powell's party lived on rancid bacon and moldy flour cakes and drank bad water. What now constitutes the great national parks of Utah, drawing millions of tourists, was once as absolutely lonely, perilous, and fear inducing as any part of Yemen or the Empty Quarter of Saudi Arabia.

Stegner writes: "Nine men had plunged into the unknown from the last outpost of civilization in the Uinta Valley on the sixth of July, 1869. On August 30 six came out."[10]

They had unlocked the last great puzzle piece of the American continent: a piece so absent of firsthand inquiry that "scientific knowledge lay on the surface like the moss agates and jasper geodes of some of its valleys, ready to be scooped up in the hand," Stegner goes on. "Powell's mark was already on it. Its mountains and creeks and buttes bore names he and his men had given them." A historical chapter that had begun at the very beginning of the nineteenth century with Jefferson's Louisiana Purchase now ended seven decades later with the map of what would become the lower forty-eight states virtually complete.[11]

In the ensuing years, John Wesley Powell would play a pivotal part in the establishment of the Washington institutions designed to both study and regulate the use and settlement of the arid West. The bureaucratic power of the federal government as we know it today has its origins in such bodies as the Geological Survey, the National Park Service, the Forest Service, the Coast and Geodetic Survey, the Bureau of Standards, the Bureau of Mines, and the Reclamation Service—all connected in one way or another to the surveying of the thinly soiled West. It might even be argued that had the United States been settled from west to east, rather than from east to west as it was, a more centralizing autocracy would have taken hold. Liberty in America emerged in part because the water-rich thirteen colonies had little need of regulation. And that natural abundance extended deep into the prairie. Whereas Iowa was almost 100 percent arable, Utah, for example, had only about 3 percent arable land. Thus, pioneers could not simply overrun Utah and prosper. Strict guidelines from a centralizing state authority were required for them to thrive.

The message of Powell's land surveys would create a paradox: while the Rocky Mountain West had about it the aura of frontiersmanship and individualism, its very aridity required the public interest to override individual interest. Powell's vision meant an end to laissez-faire and emphasized communal control over irrigation— something that would dramatically increase the power of Washington. And that is exactly what happened: from the ninety-fifth meridian to the Pacific, "reclamation," as Stegner writes, "has already remade the map of the West." The great man-made dam projects (Hoover, Grand Coulee, Bonneville), the river canalizations, the artificial floodplains, and reservoirs (most famously Lake Mead) have literally changed the geography of half of the United States.[12]

The grandiose scenery of the West may have "stunned the imagination" and "detonated words of prophecy," leading to a sense of American greatness that would simply not have existed (at least not to the same extent) had the West been a mere topographical extension of the East.[13] And yet, as Stegner's recounting of the life of Wes Powell demonstrates, the western landscape cried out about dangers, limits, and facts above scenic fantasy. Though Americans and especially their intellectuals abjure such a thing as fate, the very

physical features of the continent, and the way in which the pioneers adapted to them, demonstrate that such a thing as fate exists.
We cannot always do what we want. Other forces shape our outcomes. Thus, John Wesley Powell becomes the ultimate American
hero for those like Stegner, DeVoto, and Webb. For Powell, the
only ideas were in self-evident, physical facts and practicalities.

ON THE NEBRASKA–SOUTH DAKOTA border the spooky grandeur
of the Oglala and Buffalo Gap National Grasslands breaks up into
the Black Hills, named thus by the Lakota Sioux because of the
dark pine and spruce cover of these low mountains. I pass through
a marble memorial entrance much like the monuments in Washington, D.C., and then through an open-air colonnade adorned
with the flags of the fifty states and territories, each state's name
and date of entry into the Union carved into the square pillars.
Recent immigrants, veterans from Vietnam, Iraq, and Afghanistan, and many, many others are walking toward the viewing terrace. The voices are hushed to the point almost of silence.
Everyone's eyes rise upward to the top of the mountain, where the
sixty-foot-tall heads of four presidents are carved into the granite,
like gods, "as close to heaven as we can" make them, in the words of
the sculptor, Gutzon Borglum.

Washington, Jefferson, Lincoln, and Theodore Roosevelt: the
four greatest presidents at the time of the 150th anniversary of
American independence in 1926, when Borglum began his work
here. The granite insures that the work will stand undiminished
for at least a thousand years. After I have driven across the conti-

nent into this wilderness, Mount Rushmore offers me revelations in person that all the photographs of it cannot. For Mount Rushmore overwhelms precisely because of where it is located, not on the Capitol Mall but atop a mountain in the West, part of the original Louisiana Purchase, bearing the promise of a continent that was the upshot of pioneer optimism. An optimism that, in turn, was driven by democracy and the breaking down of European elite systems that these four presidents did so much to originate and secure. The culmination of the American story—one that Washington and Jefferson began—has more to do with the West than with the East.

These carvings, despite their inhuman size, are strangely not oppressive or totemic. They do not intimidate or call to mind some tyrannical force. There is light and not darkness in the eyes of these presidents. Each is looking into the future, it seems. Borglum, well-known for his racism, anti-Semitism, and, in general, fascist tendencies, may have wanted to create something mythic and heroic rather than democratic, or to do both, but the result of the sculptor's efforts actually works in spite of his own personal ugliness. America and its history pass into myth here, but it is a myth of light that puts into some tragic perspective, at least, the darkness rained on the native inhabitants and their way of life in these same hills.

"Mountain carving," writes the British-born Columbia University art historian Simon Schama, proclaims "in the most emphatic rhetoric imaginable, the supremacy of humanity, its uncontested possession of nature." It is about dominance, in other words. Schama compares Borglum's artistic values to those of the Nazi builder Albert Speer. Schama believes that American democracy is better represented by "the drab, often picayune wranglings of Congress than in four granite colossi carved from the side of a mountain." To Schama, by locating these colossi along the very mountainous "spine of the continent," Borglum is signaling, wittingly or unwittingly, "America's true essence: its territorial expansiveness."[14] Of course, in terms of artistic values, Schama's takedown of Borglum has much validity. But simply because Mount Rushmore does not meet the standards of the aesthetic connoisseur does not mean that it is without value: in the same way that John Philip Sousa's rousing and pompous marching music—the songs my father loved so much—which certainly does not rise to the level of Mozart or Beethoven, can nevertheless inspire wholesome patriotic feeling.

The drab workings of Congress may be a better monument to democracy than Mount Rushmore. But institutions such as Congress, with all its gridlock and unsatisfying, albeit necessary, compromises, cannot regularly inspire the common man. A Mount Rushmore is needed. It fills a void. People just feel better about their country after they see it, that's all. And who says that Mount Rushmore has to be judged as art, anyway? It exists outside art—not as something bigger or better, but simply in another category. Art criticism, by its nature, cannot account for geopolitics; so, I ask, would the world as a whole be better off without America's "territorial expansiveness," however morally unjustifiable it has been in key instances?

Meanwhile, in the adjacent tourist trap of Keystone, South Dakota, many of the waiters and waitresses are from places as diverse as Ukraine, India, Nepal, and so on. They are trying to make it and stay in America—yes, still the land of opportunity. Whereas at the viewing terrace there was whispering and outright silence, here the tourists—who include immigrants from Asia and Latin America—are all chattering away, exchanging notes and competing with one another to tell just how far and through how many states they traveled in order to get here. The license plates in the parking lots are from every part of the country. Keystone, snaking and ramshackle, is like a vast hostelry at an ancient pilgrimage site. The great and nearby monument has shown them what they all have in common.

I see the arc of my journey here. It has a purpose. There is nothing eccentric about driving slowly, for weeks on end, from one side of the continent to the other. Keystone reveals to me exactly what I am doing, since what I am looking for actually exists.

WHERE DOES THE UNITED STATES fit in the geographical history of the world? I ask myself while driving from western North Dakota into eastern Wyoming, observing the rippling, take-your-breath-away sagebrush grasslands. As I've mentioned, the United States represents the last resource-rich part of the temperate zone to be settled by Europeans during and following the Enlightenment. Temperate-zone North America is also the greatest of the geographical satellites protected by oceans from the "World-Island" of Afro-Eurasia, as early-twentieth-century British geographer Halford Mackinder called the Eastern Hemisphere. European civilization had a perfect, protected position here, as well as an abundance of inland waterways and natural resources not found on such a scale anywhere else. This has provided the United States, once

Lincoln defeated the Rebellion, with latent geographical and political power heretofore unknown in history.

The fact that World War II decimated the landscapes and infrastructures of both Europe and Asia, leaving America unscathed, only punctuates how geography has blessed the United States. Americans, especially their political and intellectual elites, can discount geography only because they have not been the victims of it like other peoples—and even as so much of their own past and historical sites are associated with it. In Poland, Romania, the Philippines, Vietnam, and other places that I have visited as a journalist, I have always heard the lament *Geography is our nightmare.* Not here—here there is black soil, underground geological riches, sprawling wilderness, and protective oceans. And this bounty changed utterly the European settlers—politically, psychologically, and philosophically—turning them into Americans, with the Great Plains providing the most vivid example.

But the combination of urbanization, advancing technology, and absolute rises in population, along with a plethora of other changes at home and abroad, wears away, much faster than the eons of wind and rain on the granite monuments, the advantages that geography confers: throwing us back on our own qualities as a society and political culture, both the good and the bad. The competition is less and less fixed in our favor. Yes, it is true that technology shrinks geography, making it both more precious and vulnerable as a consequence. Enemies can get at us in a way they couldn't in earlier periods, forcing us to be more ensnared by the world. But days of driving through this high semidesert indicate just how abstract and distant the outside world can also seem. Barring a mass casualty attack, a war gone horribly wrong, a disease pandemic, or some other such thing, many Americans have too little concrete evidence of the dangers outside that those in Washington must grapple with on a daily basis.

AT A STUFFY ONE-ROOM RESTAURANT in Fort Laramie, Wyoming, there is a life-size cardboard cutout of a female fighter jet pilot, announcing a 10 percent discount for active duty military. As I've said, highways everywhere in the West are dedicated to the armed forces. And everywhere on the road I see veterans, proudly wearing black-and-gold-lettered ball caps that declare the war they fought in, or the ship or ground unit they served with. The cans to drop your change in at the countertops in the West are not for the Humane Society but for the Veterans of Foreign Wars Auxiliary. The Iraq War may have turned out to be unpopular, but the casualty count has only deepened the public's love for the troops. Unlike Europe, where a number of countries either collaborated with the Nazis or were neutral in World War II, and saw millions perish for no obvious cause in World War I, Americans, bearing the traits of a frontier and settler society, bond with their military as in few countries on earth. The healthiest civil-military relationship among major world powers is what, at root, allows the United States to sustain high defense budgets and to posture aggressively overseas. In Europe, despite the threats of terrorism, seaborne refugees, a disintegrating Middle East next door, and a revanchist Russia, the military is often seen by civilians as merely civil servants in funny uniforms. In America, which arguably is less threatened because of the advantages that geography still bestows, a military uniform means higher social status. Because of our history from Valley Forge onward, because of the frontier experience whose memory is preserved in our western landscape, and because the South, as Faulkner realized, was among the last regions of the continent to clear the forest and thus maintain a martial culture, the attachment Americans feel to their armed force is almost romantic. The armed forces, too, are all about conquering space.

Fort Laramie, which originated as a cottonwood stockade in 1835, stood at the confluence of the Laramie and North Platte Rivers, at the western edge of the Great Plains, prior to the first foothills of the Rocky Mountains. Eventually enlarged to a series of adobe structures, it became a crossroads and jumping-off point for westward expansion and a base for military operations during the Indian Wars later in the nineteenth century. At one point in time or another, Indians, fur trappers, mountain men, missionaries, gold seekers, cowboys, pioneers, homesteaders, Pony Express riders, and Mormons met up at this trading post and securer of trails into the mountains. Here is where Francis Parkman began his traveler's investigations and writings about Indian life, which are, in turn, detailed and critiqued in DeVoto's books. The exhibits make clear that less than 2 percent of white immigrant deaths in the West can be attributed to Indian violence. Both cultures feared open warfare, until the flood of pioneers became too great to ignore, exacerbated as it was by the discovery of gold in the nearby Indian lands of the Black Hills. Actually, Fort Laramie was less a fort than a sprawling settlement. There are the enlisted barracks, the officers' quarters, the surgeon's house bespeaking a faux-Victorian comfort, and so on. One exhibit calls it the "Ellis Island" of the immigrant pioneers who settled the West. The fort, ransacked by the winds at more than four thousand feet in altitude, is still virtually in the midst of nowhere. Even today, the edge of the High Plains can seem barely conquered.

The pioneers themselves likened the High Plains to a dry-land ocean. As I drive westward, I keep climbing in altitude. This ocean becomes increasingly turbulent, rumbling skyward into the clouds in long brown and bleached-green rolls, with sagebrush the only prominent vegetation. The clouds slide away like the dissipation of candle smoke, and iron-red sandstone ridges appear on the horizon, clarifying the vast distances. The Alcova Dam on Wyoming Route 220 is the first of the great hydraulic construction projects, built by the administration of Franklin Delano Roosevelt during the Great Depression, that I will encounter. Soon low and somber mountains, creased by evergreens, erupt into snowy granite spires. To pass through such monstrous immensities and find the soft landscape of fecund Oregon or, in the case of the Mormons, to find an even more inhospitable wilderness in the Great Basin of Greater Utah and actually to settle there—to do this was to emerge as a people who harbored an almost proprietary hold on destiny. Wallace Stegner, Roderick Frazier Nash, and others have noted that from the Puritans onward, European settlers pushing out into the wilderness of North America have often equated its geography with hope itself.

The historical markers, the local brochures, and the thumbnail histories inside the bar and restaurant menus in Wyoming refer to the Oregon, California, and Mormon Trail pioneers as "the immigrants": for settling the West represented a risk, a desperate adventure, and a radical cultural adjustment almost as much as crossing the Atlantic from Europe did. To consider the settlement of the West as the essential immigrant experience is to have a more aggressive, taming-the-frontier view of American exceptionalism than those who see America as merely the antithesis to Europe, with the latter's Old World prejudices. Taming the frontier is implicitly imperial. Again, both sensibilities are necessary to operate across the globe as the United States does, and to do so within certain moral boundaries. The actual Ellis Island immigrant experience saw America as a refuge; the westering pioneer immigrant experience saw America as an ideal built on conquest.

Jeffrey City, Wyoming, used to be a thriving uranium mining town until the 1980s, when the need for uranium suddenly dropped off, amid environmental controversies and other concerns. Now people sit at a derelict café here and customers file in to buy cigarettes. Throughout the settlements of eastern and central Wyoming I see stores where the biggest signs are for cigarettes, chewing tobacco, and guns. For example: "The Armory at Able Tactical" offers "firearms, ammunition, outdoor equipment, gunsmithing." The gun culture is an extension of the frontier culture, and the frontier culture survives in extremely low population zones like this. In geographical terms, the *red* frontier culture dominates large swaths of the United States, not only in the Great Plains and Rocky Mountains but also in the South. But in demographic terms—in voting terms—it is slowly shrinking. Still, to a sizable class of white males, disappointed in life and disoriented in a changing world civilization, the gun and the pickup truck now provide the basis for identity and self-respect. To drive across America as I am doing is to go usefully back in time, in order to gain a certain perspective absent in the crowded East—but back in time, nevertheless. The world that these men yearn for will not come back. The geographic immensities are right here, but the demographic ones are at airport hubs, in the cities, and in the sprawling suburbs, where far fewer people smoke, fewer are obese, and far more people feel themselves immersed in a global civilization.

THIS IS A RADICAL FRONTIER landscape still. Faulkner's geographic determinism, an aspect of his writing, is still with us. And yet if the South (and the West, too) provide us with tragedy, at the same time the western wilderness with its prairies, plains, and mountains has provided Americans with a basis for their international ambition. *For if this unending vastness could be conquered, then, after some fashion, the world could be, too.*

Originally, the wilderness provided the setting for a big vision of federal authority: management of forest and water resources, with great dams and turnpikes to follow. That vision, though not actualized until the late nineteenth century and early decades of the twentieth, was something that in very rudimentary form Lincoln understood, with his uncompromising belief in national unity from the beginning of his presidency. Landscape power became economic power and indirectly education power, as the dozens of state universities demonstrate. And economic power means unending social turbulence, with unfairness and disparities everywhere, the upshot of dynamism itself: this is not to justify or to accept such inequalities but merely to put them in some perspective. And these inequalities over a vast landscape pull Americans and their leaders back into the continent, where so much remains to be fixed or ameliorated. It's complicated. And because it is complicated, our leaders in Washington are enjoined to be centrists and pragmatists who should not want to conquer the world—yet should not want to withdraw from it either. I respect the innate isolationist impulse of the interior continent, where few want to discuss politics and certainly not foreign policy: not so much because such discussions are radioactive (after all, polls show that people living in the same states and counties often agree with one another on these things); rather, they avoid such discussions because they are removed from their immediate concerns.

But I also know that America has been on a long journey, away from its own history and toward becoming enmeshed in a global history. The irony is that to be effective globally, American leaders must be anchored to their own soil. It is their own soil—the landscape through which I now pass, overpowering and largely empty— that alone can properly orient them.

WYOMING'S SOUTH PASS, the Continental Divide, a plateau more than 7,500 feet in altitude: it comes upon you after the earth has shattered into a chaos of deformed, snow-flecked ridges. There is almost nothing to look at now but the sky. Here is the most significant gateway through the Rockies, the one through which the Mormons traveled. It is a prelude to the terrifying natural stage set of Utah and the Great Basin stretching into northern Arizona,

Nevada, and California. Now begins the eruption of the Wasatch, Uinta, and other ranges. It is an overwhelming scenery that obliterates human time and thus helped to confirm to the Latter-day Saints that they were indeed on a spiritual mission beyond normal history. Yes, American exceptionalism can be insufferable, but it is partly a product of landscape.

And conquering that landscape, conquering not only space but nature and inhuman time in a manner of speaking, was something that was done by altering the landscape itself in many places. As I drive across Flaming Gorge Dam in northeastern Utah, on one side of the rim is a placid reservoir of colossal proportions; on the other side a dizzying precipice of poured concrete that drops five hundred feet to the bottom, built between 1956 and 1964 under three American presidents. The vermilion rocks that caused John Wesley Powell to name it Flaming Gorge are now submerged beneath the reservoir. The Green River system, down which Powell and his party risked repeated destruction—in negotiating one long and angry sequence of rapids after another—is now docile and tamed.

You have to come to the town of Green River in east-central Utah in order to appreciate John Wesley Powell's bravery and achievement. You drive for a while south of Salt Lake City on the interstate, then strike out east for 125 miles into the semidesert. In the pellucid air of five to seven thousand feet, the tortured shapes of the curving canyons—salmon, vermilion, fiery lava, sulfur, white zinc, and cindery black; buttes, mesas, and monuments—show you a potter's landscape with the whole panoply of earthen shades. Here and there I happen upon a small town, or more specifically an assemblage of gas stations and convenience stores. Finally the Green River appears, cutting through the parched immensity. The town is a bit larger than the others, thanks to a few motels. Powell's party had launched themselves into an unmapped wilderness, a wilderness that is still palpable. This place was the last stage in consolidating a continental empire. But the deeper and far more relevant message of Powell's discoveries—the one he would want us to remember—is that the very aridity of this landscape, where the river itself is the only life-sustaining element unto the horizon, argues for restraint, planning, and humility in much of what we do, domestic and foreign. Despite technology, relatively few can live here even now.

THE WESTERN LANDSCAPE OVERWHELMS by its very repetition of ranges and canyons. Your mind wanders, as there is no human habitation in view to constitute a focal point. Your thoughts become more abstract. There are fewer and fewer conversations to overhear. I see before me the vision of the Hudson River School, a group of painters that emerged in the middle of the nineteenth century, depicting the landscape of New York's Hudson River valley, along with the adjacent Catskill and Adirondack Mountains. In following generations, their subject matter spread eastward to the landscapes of the New England coast and westward to the Rocky Mountains and Sierra Nevada. Their work was the equivalent in brushstrokes of Henry David Thoreau's and Ralph Waldo Emerson's transcendentalism. The panoramic landscapes of Thomas Cole, Albert Bierstadt, Frederic Edwin Church, and others of the

Hudson River School evoke lucidity, silence, primitiveness, and an iconic, almost photographic clarity. They were painting paradise, in other words, giving a sense of the biblical or Delphic majesty—take your pick—to the American landscape and consequently invoking meditation upon it. In its very wildness, this natural landscape ran closely parallel to all the possibilities associated with political freedom. And because all the backdrops were American, the reverence of these painters for this landscape supplied a distinctive artistic layer to the country's emerging nationalism (though perhaps without their meaning to). Adding to the poignancy of this scenic art was the threat of industrialization and the initial stirrings of the mass society that the nineteenth century brought with it, from which these idyllic wilderness backdrops constituted a respite. These artistic creations signify a singular American aesthetic. The paintings of the Hudson River School might as well accompany DeVoto's and Stegner's prose. These paintings scream aloud Robert Frost's poem "The Gift Outright": the gift being that of a majestic landscape that challenges the occupants to create a great nation upon it.[15] Here is where patriotism and environmentalism flow together. Of course, just as the Hudson River School and the conservation movement that grew out of it—and that included Stegner and DeVoto—were patriotic responses to industrialization, the postindustrial world of megacities and exurbs has thus far spawned a postnational environmentalism that, in its sense of alienation from society, has produced a challenge to traditional patriotism.

But even the vision of the Hudson River painters was not all-encompassing. At least, that was the opinion of Walt Whitman, who believed America was great precisely because of its uncouth fury and social turbulence—its unmade, unrefined quality, which these pacific artists simply did not capture (though, to be fair, it was not their intention to do so).[16] Whitman's belief was that immigrants would remake the country into a tumultuous world civilization spanning the Pacific and other oceans, as "the principle of individuality" gradually erased cultural differences.[17] America would *become* the world, in other words, and would therefore require a larger, definable purpose in that world in order to preserve its national identity—and to keep using the terms *our* and *we,* albeit less often.

ZION NATIONAL PARK IN SOUTHWESTERN UTAH, with its towering, creamy, sky-breaking sandstone monuments, is the summation of the western landscape. The original name of the park was "Mukuntuweap," meaning "straight canyon" in the Southern Paiute language. "Zion" was chosen in 1918 as a marketing tool, in reference to the Mormons. But these are historic Indian lands, and one day the name of the park may revert accordingly, as happened to Mount McKinley, renamed Denali. In order to fully comprehend itself as a liberal world power, the United States will have to continue to come to terms with the crimes of its past. That way it will be imperial not in spirit, but only in terms of comparisons with other powers in history.

Zion's landscape is otherworldly, but at this point I have run out of adjectives. It is hard not to repeat yourself as one geological miracle succeeds another for hundreds and thousands of miles west of the Missouri. But the visitors to the park require a word or two. This is no longer the throng of clean-cut American families instilling patriotism in their children through a visit to one of the national parks. The tourists are much more varied than that: many Europeans first of all, and among the Americans many young outdoor enthusiasts with all manner of expensive and complex gear. Just as DeVoto's and Stegner's conservationist mind-set, with its emphasis on America's own history, has evolved into a planetary environmentalism, Zion National Park now has a distinctly postnational feel to it. Another thing: as at Valley Forge and other historical sites, there are quite a few Asian and Indian immigrant families here; far fewer African Americans. Given the anguish of our history, immigrants may more easily embrace it than those who are the descendants of slaves and consequently the victims of it.

I AM DRIVING ALONG the Old Spanish Trail in southern Nevada, a route that more or less horizontally crossed the Southwest. The tacky, shack-like encampments offer fireworks, cigarettes, gun advertisements, and one-arm bandits. The American West now presents itself in all of its emptiness and lack of water. Here in the Southwest, whose landscape with its slag heaps and ashen cliffs reminds me of nothing so much as Mesopotamia or Afghanistan or Yemen, America is not a natural empire at all—it is a contingent, rapacious one, living still on the edge. It is a desert culture, with the bright lights, gambling, music, and air-conditioning acting as life support systems. Much of this territory fills out the Lower 48 only because the United States won a military and political contest with

Mexico in the nineteenth century: to repeat, another morally am-
biguous legacy that later helped the country right the world in two
great wars in the century following. With Spanish-language culture surging back, as it has been for decades now, traditional American Protestant culture is not only being made more nuanced by a
new global cosmopolitan culture but by a specifically Old World,
Counter-Reformation Catholic culture to the south, furthering
America's dissolution into the planetary maelstrom. Here I feel as
if I am on unsteady ground, as if the borders of the continent are
not natural at all.

   Mexico's population, which has risen around sixfold since 1940,
is approximately a third of the population of the United States,
even as the population south of the border continues to grow at a
faster rate. Meanwhile, northern Mexico's population has more
than doubled since the signing of the 1994 North American Free
Trade Agreement with the United States. Halfway from the border
south to Mexico City, for hundreds of miles, the U.S. dollar is a
common unit of exchange. A new region-state is coming into
being, comprising northern Mexico and the southwestern United
States. This is not about America's decline or degeneration, since
Mexico itself is becoming a more dynamic, first world economy,
but about America's transformation away from its temperate-zone,
geographically based roots.

POWELL AND HIS MEN entered the Colorado River near here in
1869. In 1928, Congress and President Calvin Coolidge approved
the building of what would later be called the Hoover Dam, after

Herbert Hoover, who followed Coolidge in the White House. The dam was dedicated by President Franklin Roosevelt in 1935. Before the dam could even be built, four tunnels, each between 3,500 and 4,300 feet long, with diameters of 56 feet and 3-foot-thick walls, had to be built to divert the Colorado River. A mobile, double-decker drilling rig was invented for the purpose. The four tunnels were completed in nineteen months, two years ahead of schedule. Next came the construction of a temporary earthen dam to force the water into the diversion tunnels. To build the actual dam, mud, silt, and sand had to be excavated down 135 feet merely to reach the bedrock that would support the final colossus. The Hoover Dam is the largest arch gravity dam in the Western Hemisphere, meaning sheer force holds the water in place. On one side, near the top of its 1,244-foot span, is the creation of the dam itself, Lake Mead, 110 miles long, held back by what is on the other side of the crest; interlocking concrete aggregate blocks weighing 1,100 tons each that reach down 726.4 feet, more than the Washington Monument or the Gateway Arch in St. Louis. A million acres of farmland in several southwestern states are irrigated thanks to the Hoover Dam. The dam also supplies the domestic water needs of many millions of people in Las Vegas, Los Angeles, San Diego, Phoenix, and Tucson. The dam complex's cantilever towers that feed electricity into all the adjacent power stations sprawling over this desert—like the signs of some alien civilization—literally light up the Southwest. A loud voice recording at the dam proclaims that in the shadow of the Hoover Dam you feel that "the future is limitless," that there is nothing that man cannot achieve if he but summons the will.

I was not so sure.

The Hoover Dam, one of the great engineering wonders of the modern world, created the Southwest as we know it today. But there is a fundamental difference between this work of man and other gargantuan projects built by other empires and civilizations. Great hydraulic works, terrifying feats of monument building, and engineering projects throughout history have usually been the product of tyrannies, and therefore the work of slaves. Slaves did not build the Hoover Dam. Proud and free men built this behemoth. They competed fiercely for the well-paid jobs, like the "high-scalers," construction workers suspended nine hundred feet from the canyon rim to work on the dam. The Hoover Dam carries an entirely different meaning than many other comparable construction works throughout history.

Indeed, geography is only half the story of America. The other half is what this book does not concern itself with: the ingenuity of a European civilization, characterized by a secular Protestant creed and early modern and modern British parliamentary traditions, which were retooled here to create a degree of economic efficiency and social dynamism that is virtually unprecedented in a large democratic state. All of this went into the building of the Hoover Dam, an engineering feat that now tempts hubris.

The very death and vibrating heat exuded by this ashen landscape makes me wonder, though. Lake Mead itself is beginning to dry up, reaching historically low levels, with a soap ring forming around the edges. This will substantially reduce the amount of electricity generated by the Hoover Dam. A years-long drought is only partially the cause. The underlying factor is that the civilization of the American Southwest, including the Los Angeles–San

Diego urban corridor, does not live within sustainable limits. Too many lawns and golf courses and too much overuse of domestic water. The future may actually not be limitless. American civilization may start to contract here.

THE UNCEASING JUNGLE in the Nevada desert of absurd, crooked, corroded, pulsing neon signs advertising gambling and related entertainments stops suddenly, as another sign announces, "Welcome to California." The desert is once again pristine, something further enhanced by the mirrored, futuristic magnificence of the Ivanpah Solar Power Facility, built only a few years ago and in its own way almost as visually stunning as the Hoover Dam—as though the creation of a more advanced, alien civilization. The Hoover Dam, evidently, already has its successors, testimony to American ingenuity, and yes, an extension of the frontier ethos.

Barstow, California, is in the midst of the Mojave Desert, a cindery wilderness bleak beyond imagining. My father used to reminisce about crossing the southwestern desert, while looking at the walls of the bedroom in our apartment as if still blinded by the sun. The hotel here is bordered by the bus station and dusty outlet stores. The one-story tract homes and low-end chains generate the aura of an archaeological site, as if the town will one day soon be abandoned. Dining out gets no better than Chili's. Some of the clientele, I can tell from the conversations—so banal and technical—are contractors at the nearby Fort Irwin National Training Center, where the U.S. Army prepares for present and future battles, from set-piece engagements to counterinsurgency:

the landscape here is conducive to imagining the Middle East. In the restaurant, there are families and extended families, too, and young people. Everyone is naturally polite and speaks in low voices despite the music. As flimsy as the surroundings are, the social glue appears firm and wholesome even. The lack of aesthetics fits with America's inherent practicality, which culminates in the strip mall, the defining urban design of Barstow.

I am almost at the Pacific now, yet I am still in the midst of a tenuous desert culture. The landscape here is no friend to nationhood. The nation has been created farther back, earlier in my journey, where the prairie meets the Great Plains, and has had enough force to extend itself here, and then only by later working backward from the Pacific. Even so, the spaces between have not been filled in: rather, linear arteries of civilization have been forged from one point to another. The social glue at Chili's is the culmination of this entire process.

Indeed, Barstow was the southwestern outpost of the Mormon Corridor, a stop on the Old Spanish Trail, a place where the army encountered the Paiutes, and where the Union Pacific Railroad first met up with several interstates at the halfway point between Las Vegas and Los Angeles. This makes Barstow a transport hub for the Greater Los Angeles suburban sprawl stretching east into the desert, which is otherwise known as the Inland Empire. Of course, these are ready-made, disparate facts available from any encyclopedia. What unites them is that they all—the trail, the railways, the roads—have to do with the final imperial occupation, settlement, and development of the temperate-zone continent. Here is where, for the first time in my journey, I feel the immediacy of the Mexican border at the country's southwestern extremity. Though conquest is not pretty, power is relative. Whatever moral and geopolitical contradictions there are in America's cartographic situation and how it came to be, America's domestic condition is far more advantageous and, yes, moral compared to those of Europe, Russia, China, or India in the early twenty-first century.

In Barstow, a half-day's drive from the Pacific and from the Mexican border, I thought about America's competitors.

EUROPE, SEVENTY YEARS AFTER the beginning of the postwar unification project, is bedeviled by internal contradictions based, at root, on geography, history, language, and ethnicity. The development patterns of northern Europe, Mediterranean Europe, and Balkan Europe are still very much distinct, no matter the exceptions. European Union members Greece and Bulgaria, for example, are destitute third world countries in comparison to Germany and France. Because of these vast differences, European states still make decisions overwhelmingly on national interest rather than on any pan-European interest. The Eurocrats in Brussels may think in terms of *Europe,* but the European *street* thinks otherwise. Meanwhile, to the east, Europe is threatened by Russian aggression abroad and Russian weakness at home, with all of its disintegrative tendencies; to the southeast Europe is threatened by a chaotic and radicalized Middle East; and to the south by migrants from North Africa and sub-Saharan Africa both, as Europe's southern border is not the Mediterranean—which is really a connector—but the Sahara Desert. Europe's era of internal cohesion may already be past.

Russia covers half the longitudes of the earth, an area nearly unfeasible to unite. It is further disunited by wide rivers that flow vertically rather than diagonally, unlike the rivers that cross the American continent. Thus, Russia has been nearly impossible to govern except by the most ruthless central control. Russia has few defensible borders, which makes it the ultimate insecure land power. Throughout history, this has caused Russia to be particularly aggressive. Autocracy has come naturally to Russia the way democracy has to the United States. As deterministic as all this sounds, there are few indications that Russia's political future will be much brighter than its past. Its population is declining, except for the Muslim and other minority elements, and President Vladimir Putin's most significant political enemies are to his nationalistic right, not to his democratic-trending left.

China, unlike Russia, occupies the temperate latitudes like the United States. It has thousands of miles of coastline in the east and reaches toward energy- and mineral-rich Central Asia in the west. Its pace of development over more than a third of a century has been breathtaking—like that of the United States between the end of the Civil War and the outbreak of the Spanish-American War, the war that first announced the United States as an imperial power. But whereas the United States is the neighbor of two oceans and a sparsely populated, middle-class Canada, with only populous and still-poverty-racked Mexico as a geographic challenge, China must deal with nearby American allies Japan, South Korea, the Philippines, Australia, and so on. And this is not to mention Russia, China's historical adversary, or the unstable and nuclear-armed totalitarian state of North Korea. Even within their borders, the

Han Chinese face off against longtime historical enemies: Turkic Muslim Uighurs, Tibetans, and Inner Mongolians. China is an authoritarian state that fears political liberalization because, among other things, it could lead to more unrest in these minority areas. Still, such increasing unrest may be unavoidable because whatever problems the U.S. economy has, and however unbalanced the distribution of wealth is inside the United States, China's economic tribulations—coming off its long boom—are far more profound and structural. No, China is not about to supplant the United States as the greatest world power. And even if it could, the argument that a Chinese-dominated world would be safer and more humane than an American-dominated one is, frankly, weak to the point of absurdity.

India possesses eminent geographic logic, framed as it is by the Arabian Sea, Bay of Bengal, Burmese jungles, and the Himalayan mountain system. Nevertheless, India has lacked a singular building block of demographic organization like China's Wei Valley and lower Yellow River. India's river system, in general, divides more than it unites. India's tropical latitudes coupled with the history of invasions from the northwest have historically weakened governing continuity and economic development. Of course, India is politically stable, manifestly democratic, and driven by a national purpose. India has great possibilities. It can be a great pivot power in twenty-first-century politics. But it simply lacks the capacity to truly compete or overtake the United States in the near- or middle-term future.

This is all obvious enough. But it must be mentioned simply in order to demonstrate that at least in terms of conventional geopolitics, the United States still has no real competitors. Geography remains an overwhelming advantage and source of American power. I have traveled for many weeks from east to west across the most impressive political geography in the world, or in history for that matter.

I CROSS ANOTHER SERIES of mountains before the faint rinse of sea air clarifies the landscape. A global city-state suddenly appears like the ones I left behind on the other coast: this time with thin, sun-tanned people; traffic jams; and a well-manicured, unending sub-urbia. Reaching the San Diego harbor, I spot a line of gigantic gray-hulled warships in their berths, facing toward the rest of the world.

CATHAY

THERE ARE FEW SINGULAR EXPRESSIONS OF MILITARY AND NATIONAL power in the early twenty-first century as vivid as that of Naval Base San Diego, the principal port in the Lower 48 of the U.S. Pacific Fleet. Witness the miles of more than fifty gray-hulled steel behemoths of war, each surface ship and submarine costing billions of dollars, lined up, as if in formation, in their gargantuan piers: frigates, destroyers, cruisers, amphibs, and the odd aircraft carrier—a single carrier costing upward of $18 billion, with its dozens of fighter jets and other squadrons on deck. Each of the navy's eleven Nimitz- and Ford-class nuclear-powered supercarriers, with a flight deck several football fields in length, is an icon of imperial-like maintenance: able to launch air attacks on shore from hundreds of miles away; able, simply by virtue of its location at sea, to apply diplomatic pressure while keeping the guns silent. Indeed, a lone U.S. aircraft carrier strike group, with its train of cruisers, destroyers, submarine, and other ships, constitutes (excepting nu-clear bombs) the foremost weapon of violent destruction of the modern and postmodern ages. The United States has more than double the number of aircraft carriers of any other country, and many of its closest competitors have carriers that the U.S. Navy would not even label carriers at all—to us, they would be smaller amphibious assault ships.

This is the industrial-age navy that Theodore Roosevelt began to build more than a century ago with his Great White Fleet—the navy battle fleet that circumnavigated the globe from 1907 to 1909 in order to advance his imperial vision. Because the actual use of nuclear weapons is (to say the least) extremely problematic, it is this navy, since the end of World War II, that has constituted America's most important strategic instrument.

After more than a month of driving, I see the coastline in full force, underlining the distance that I traveled. Leaving my car to look closer at these ships, I recall that in the estimation of the Yale-and Cambridge-educated historian and archaeologist John R. Hale, it was the Athenian navy that was the "emblem of liberty and democracy," as well as of "imperial ambition," governing 150 is-lands and coastal city-states. "Without the Athenian navy," Hale writes, "there would have been no Parthenon, no tragedies of Sophocles or Euripides, no *Republic* of Plato or *Politics* of Aristotle." The warships of ancient Athens were "also a force that fostered new democracies throughout the Greek world."[1] It is not an exag-geration to say that the U.S. Navy has served a similar function—if not quite to the same degree—throughout this country's history and especially since the 1940s.

It is this navy, organized basically into aircraft carrier strike groups, working in unison with America's numbered air forces, that sustains a liberal maritime order, in which sea lines of communication and access to hydrocarbons are secure for America's allies, with piracy confined to the edges of the battlespace as an exotic nuisance only. Such is the primary geopolitical good that America provides the world. While American soldiers and marines have fought and died in dirty, unconventional wars, it is these warships—the silent guardians of freedom—that, helped by air support, project power across large swaths of the earth on a daily basis. America may have been humbled in Afghanistan and Iraq, where fixing complex Islamic societies on the ground has proved out of reach, but U.S. power is still primarily registered by its navy and air force, whether or not they gather headlines. While our land forces are for unpredictable contingencies, our sea and air forces secure the global commons. The navy is our *away team:* its operations tempo around the world is the same, whether in peacetime or wartime. So crucial is our navy that were just one of America's eleven aircraft carriers sunk or disabled by an enemy combatant, it would constitute a national disaster in strategic and reputational terms as devastating as 9/11. Manifest Destiny, the conquest of a continent with its unleashing of vast economic wealth and national will, reaches a point of concision here at Naval Base San Diego. It is a fitting end to my journey.

In the previous decade, I spent many weeks as a journalist sailing across the Pacific and through the Indonesian archipelago aboard the USS *Benfold,* an Arleigh Burke–class guided missile destroyer home-ported here at San Diego. I spent more weeks in the Pacific aboard the USS *Houston,* a Los Angeles–class nuclear attack submarine home-ported at Pearl Harbor in Hawaii. In each case I was living among hundreds of sailors in their early and mid-twenties, inside a cramped, gray space bobbing up and down through an oceanic immensity: truly, the Pacific is incomprehensibly vast when you are crawling across it at thirty knots or so. Those young men and women often hailed from the flat, yawning interior of the continent—stretching from the easternmost prairie to the westernmost High Plains, the same areas through which I have traveled—and had never seen an ocean until they joined the navy. Yet the conquest of *space* was in their psyche, as if inherited from their ancestors, and they collaborated in perfect harmony, mastering the most complex feats of electronic warfare and mechanical rigors of seamanship. A crew of three-hundred-plus sailors and officers on each destroyer, on each submarine, cruiser, and so on, all must coordinate with the five-thousand-member crew aboard a carrier. These are like small towns at sea. American naval power is built not only on hardware, but on generations of tradition without which such hardware could not be operated. We conquered a dry-land continent, water-starved in its desert reaches, in order to become a maritime nation.

GEOGRAPHY IS NOT WHERE analysis of national power ends, but it is surely where it begins. The fact is, America's geography is the most favored in the world: one perfectly apportioned for nationhood and global responsibility. Whereas Alaska and Hawaii allow the United States to project power all across the northern and central Pacific, the lower forty-eight states are protected by two great oceans and the Canadian Arctic: it is only Mexico to the south, with its comparatively young (agewise) population of 122 million, buttressed by even younger populations in Central America, that inhibits to a limited extent America's combination of splendid isolation and oceanic access to both Europe and Asia.

It is a continent endowed with forests and fertile land, not to mention deposits of iron, coal, lead, silver, and gold (and, as it would turn out in the second half of the nineteenth century, hydrocarbons). More crucially, though, and lesser realized, the Lower 48 boast more miles of navigable inland waterways than much of the rest of the world put together. As we've already seen, the Mississippi, Missouri, Ohio, Arkansas, and Tennessee river systems flow diagonally rather than perpendicularly across the continent, thereby uniting the entire temperate zone of North America—which happens to be overwhelmingly occupied by the United States. And this inland river network, to repeat, rather than flow primarily across America's desert portions, is mainly laid over the continent's arable cradle—the rich soil of the Middle West—encouraging the movement of people as well as allowing produce to more easily get to market, opening up the continental interior to exploration and trade.[2] There is, too, the continent's frequently indented coastline with its protected, natural deep water ports, particularly on the East Coast, which allowed for the robust economic development of the original thirteen colonies in the first place. Moreover, on the East and Gulf Coasts, there are long barrier islands, protecting in places this indented seaboard, which foster shipping from one part of the continent to another. All these factors further enhance the commercial power of America's river systems, for which the great Mississippi is a funnel, emptying into the Gulf of Mexico and the Caribbean.

Indeed, it was geography that set the stage for a hemispheric empire. The great Dutch American strategist of the 1930s and early 1940s, Nicholas Spykman, explained that by gaining effective control of the Greater Caribbean, the blue-water extension of its continental landmass, the United States came to dominate the Western Hemisphere, and with that had resources to spare to affect the balance of power in the Eastern Hemisphere. And that proved to be the essential geopolitical dynamic of the twentieth century, as the United States tipped the balance of forces in its favor in two world wars and the Cold War that followed. This all had to do with many things, obviously, but without such a fortuitous geography those troop trains near Cairo, Illinois, that my father saw converging in 1942 would have been inconceivable.

The geographic shorthand of the lower forty-eight states is the following: The original colonies hugging the Eastern Seaboard were blessed by many good natural harbors, even as the Appalachian Mountains to the west provided for a protective barrier in the early stages of settlement. That protective barrier, however, was marked by valleys through which settlers could pass into the midwestern prairie, a flat panel of cultivation that engendered the building of a unique American culture by erasing the differences among immigrant communities through productive labor. By the time westering pioneers met a truly formidable geographical barrier—the Great American Desert—the joining of an already strong national identity with the technology that built, among other things, the transcontinental railroad allowed for the culmination of Manifest Destiny. Americans are a great people not only because of their democracy and their Protestant creed (uniting faith in one god with hard work, which all non-Protestant immigrants unconsciously adopt), but also because of where they happen to live.

Because this unprecedented geographic bounty has allowed the United States to both dominate the Western Hemisphere and help determine events in the Eastern Hemisphere, America, by virtue of its location, has interests throughout Eurasia, from Europe to China. If, as I must repeat, you think of Afro-Eurasia as the "World-Island," in the words of the great British imperial geographer Halford Mackinder, then North America is the greatest of the satellite landmasses able to influence that World-Island.[3] The swollen vein of the Mississippi, accepting the capillaries of the other river systems of the heartland with all of their commerce, pours out into the Greater Caribbean and, in turn, into the great oceans (later helped by the Panama Canal), establishing for the United States since the mid-nineteenth century the kernel of an abiding interest in all the other continents, which share those same oceans.

The world of today offers a granular tableau of American involvement. That involvement, whether well conceived or badly conceived, wise or unwise, all radiates, however indirectly, from our blessed continental situation. We have never been a formal empire, despite intermittent imperial interludes such as governing (or helping to found) Liberia, the Philippines, postwar Japan and Germany, and so on. But our worldwide influence, our military and diplomatic challenges, and our general frustrations, particularly in Afro-Eurasia, are of imperial-like dimensions: meaning that any historical comparisons regarding our international situation must be with former empires, even if we hate to call ourselves imperial. We struggle diplomatically and through our military deployments to prevent the kind of domination of the Eastern Hemisphere by a rival power that we ourselves enjoy in the Western Hemisphere. This is an amoral endeavor that achieves a moral result. It has meant that we support the democracies and social welfare states of Europe against an illiberal, revanchist Russia, and the democratic and capitalist states of South and East Asia against an authoritarian and bullying China. The Soviet Union may be dead and China may no longer be Communist per se, but Russia's and China's very size, large populations, and undemocratic governments mean that they must be balanced against, thus providing the United States with equities of some, albeit limited, value in such far-flung locales as Ukraine and Afghanistan.

All of this is the context for why it is necessary for America to manage the Pacific through the presence of the Seventh Fleet and to provide NATO in Europe with the bulk of its support. Without NATO in Europe, and without U.S. warships in the South and East China Seas—as well as in the Persian Gulf and Mediterranean—robust, venerable, and iconic democracies such as the Baltic states, Israel, and Taiwan might never have been able to survive at all. Countries like Vietnam, Malaysia, and the Philippines in South-

east Asia—as well as countries in Central and Eastern Europe—
would be Finlandized (dominated) by Beijing and Moscow. In a
larger sense, moreover, without the constellation of U.S. forces
around the world, the risk of major, interstate war would increase
substantially.

As I write, the U.S. Navy has close to three hundred warships.
Indeed, a world with only, say, two hundred American warships
would be a very different place.[4] For it is that three-hundred-ship
navy whose very stabilizing presence helps keep the peace between
Japan and China, between India and China, between the countries
of the Persian Gulf and Iran, and so on. On any given week, U.S.
Army Special Forces (Green Berets) are on training missions in
dozens of countries, mentoring host country armies not only on
how to fight, but on respecting human rights and the proper role of
militaries in fledgling democracies. The United States may have
fought unnecessary wars in Vietnam and Iraq, making situations in
those countries worse rather than better, but over the chasm of the
decades, since the mid-twentieth century, the United States,
through both its military and diplomatic service, has made the
world far less unstable and far more friendly to civil society than it
would otherwise have been. And that is to say nothing of our economic aid, both bilateral assistance and our support for international organizations such as the International Monetary Fund and
the World Bank. These facts may seem trite and commonplace. But
by the standards of imperial history reaching back to antiquity—
again, the only history with which our foreign policy bears any
comparison—these facts are extraordinary and should never be

taken for granted. The European Union and globalization itself are impossible to even contemplate without the overarching fact of American power.

Having provided the United States an unparalleled degree of protection from the turmoil of Afro-Eurasia, even as it has given America access to Atlantic and Pacific sea-lanes, this same geography has now been considerably neutralized by technology: by everything from air travel to electronic communications. This has only deepened American involvement and influence around the globe. We remain an immense continent but in an increasingly smaller and interconnected world, so that we are, more and more, vulnerable to everything from global financial disruptions to violent ideological movements. As 9/11—to take the most obvious example—demonstrated, Islamic extremism must (to say the least) be balanced against, if not eroded and contained. Thus, it is simply impossible for us to escape from the geopolitical intimacy of the twenty-first-century world.

What all of this amounts to is something stark: America is *fated to lead.* That is the judgment of geography as it has played out over the past two and a half centuries.

And there is something else.

In the course of being fated to lead for unceasing decades, the United States has incurred, like it or not, other, very unique obligations. To name just one example, there is the delicate point of the United States Holocaust Memorial Museum. The fact that this museum constitutes both a monument and historical repository is actually less significant than (as others have noted) its location, adjacent to the National Mall in Washington, D.C., practically within sight of the Jefferson Memorial. The Holocaust—something that happened to Jews in Europe—has been officially granted entry into the American historical experience, so that whenever large-scale atrocities happen anywhere, America must at the very least take notice, if not lead some sort of response.

No, America is not a normal country, as the late conservative luminary Jeane J. Kirkpatrick once suggested that it might become at the end of the Cold War. A normal country that minded its own business would not have such a museum as part of its pantheon. America, rather, has obligations of an imperial scale: again, just look at the size of its navy and air force and how their platforms are distributed around the planet. Consider that at the turn of the twenty-first century, the United States had more than seven hundred military bases of some sort in 130 countries. Even the U.S. Coast Guard, officially a nonmilitary force, is deployed in various parts of the globe and would count as the world's twelfth largest navy.

This is the material at hand with which we have no choice but to deal. Bernard DeVoto intuitively grasped it, traveling around the interior of the United States in 1940 as he did, passionately arguing in local community gatherings for America to enter the war. He loved the continent that he considered both a republic and an empire. There was just so much going on inside it that the world beyond was never quite real. In thinking this way, he saw the complex moral and geopolitical ramifications of Manifest Destiny before generations of academics would see nothing but evil in it. Truly, he grasped that the blessings of geographical fate had burdened America with global responsibilities.

So did, for example, George H. W. Bush, America's last truly nation-state president and the last president to have fought in World War II, who had elite New England prep schools, the naval war in the Pacific, and the Texas oil fields as his rite-of-passage points of reference. The elder Bush was no intellectual, but he deeply internalized exactly what the bookish DeVoto had: that America was a continent of such dimensions that to lead was not a choice, but a fate. Thus, he made incessant phone calls to world leaders from the very start of his presidency—long before the collapse of the Soviet empire and Iraq's invasion of Kuwait made such calls especially necessary. Bush's decision to commit hundreds of thousands of U.S. troops in order to eject Iraq from Kuwait smacked of the boldness associated with Manifest Destiny, just as his decisions not to break relations with China after the Tiananmen Square massacre—and not to openly beat his breast following the collapse of the Warsaw Pact—smacked of the restraints associated with the settlement of a water-starved American West. The contradictory lessons of westering settlement were unconsciously written into the logic of his foreign policy. And thus he ended up being one of America's greatest one-term presidents, not far behind James K. Polk.

Faced with such indisputable truths about the geographical circumstances of the United States, what they imply, and the lessons they teach, the debate between realists and idealists that goes on in Washington is at once unnecessarily Manichaean and a mere row over tactics. Realism wasn't the evil invention of Henry Kissinger but an American tradition in foreign policy going back to George Washington, John Quincy Adams, and "wise men" such as George

F. Kennan and Dean Acheson. Idealism, for its part, is so deeply embedded in the American tradition that Wilsonianism lives on long after the passing of America's twenty-eighth president, no matter how often it might be shown to be flawed. John Quincy Adams warned Americans not to go out in search of "monsters to destroy," but Woodrow Wilson effectively urged his countrymen to do exactly that. Thus, American foreign policy has often been a compromise between those two sensibilities. Ronald Reagan spoke the soaring rhetoric of Wilsonian moral rearmament, even as he surrounded himself with realists at the Pentagon, at the State Department, and inside the White House itself, whose advice he slyly accepted. This inherent compromise was a key element in his greatness.

Neither unremitting humanitarianism (because it is unsustainable) nor neo-isolationism (because it fails to accept America's geographical *fate* as a world leader) can be the basis of any responsible foreign policy. America's foreign policy will always be Wilsonian to some degree, in that all American presidents seek to expand the boundaries of civil society the world over. It is in the resistance to this goal, and the risk and price associated with overcoming such resistance from America's adversaries, that realists will be first among those urging restraint. Realists generally opt for interests over values, since our values cannot be imposed everywhere; they opt for order over freedom, since without order there is anarchy and therefore no freedom for anybody. Wilsonian idealists frequently clash with realists when the debate focuses on the level of intervention in this particular country and that one. But both sides, the fringes excepted, have always supported a vigorous American security and diplomatic presence the world over. And that very consensus, in a wider historical sense, overshadows the simmering philosophical debate over how to manage and employ such a presence on any given day.

American foreign policy, precisely because it is that of a great continental power, is governed by the tension between morality and amorality. Power can be spent morally in humanitarian endeavors, but that very power can only be acquired amorally for the sake of balancing against geopolitical adversaries and protecting sea lines of communication and access to hydrocarbons: goals that while not immoral, still do not necessarily fall within the category of lofty principles. Thus, continued humanitarianism requires the continued amoral acquisition and maintenance of American power. Rather than immobilize foreign policy, this uneasy dichotomy with all the arguments that it has generated has only served to further energize the policy-making elite, which is a good thing.

Let us revisit, for a moment, historian Frederick Jackson Turner's 1893 thesis, "The Significance of the Frontier in American History." Americans, he wrote, have been a restive, aggressive people formed by the need to clear the forest in their pioneering efforts. The frontier made Americans a nation on the march in a way that other peoples just were not. Because we were a frontier society, we were a settler society as well, and settler societies absorb immigrants better than societies fixed in the same terrain for hundreds and thousands of years. New land creates wider opportunities, which, in turn, break down established hierarchies.

Turner worried that the closing of the western frontier in 1890 might dilute this dynamism. Theodore Roosevelt differed, saying the country's crass materialism, to cite just one example, was a healthy sign that the frontier ethos was embedded deeply enough in the American character not to be erased. The continued American obsession with technological innovation has been another facet of the frontier ethos. And so, I would argue, is the consensus shared among both voters and Congress for decades: that American naval forces need to be deployed not just in the role of a coast guard, but everywhere around the globe.

Keep in mind that soon after the last battles of the Indian Wars were concluded in 1890, about the same time that Turner worried about the effect of the closure of the frontier on the American psyche, the U.S. Army became immediately active for three decades in Cuba, Puerto Rico, Panama, and Mexico, as well as in a number of small wars and stabilization and policing expeditions just beyond the borders of the continental United States. And this is to say nothing about similar operations during that time frame in the Philippines, China, and Siberia, all in addition to the American expeditionary force being sent to Europe to fight in World War I. Settling the continent, clearing space—a dangerous, morally blemished, and often violent endeavor that took several centuries, depending upon how you count—insured that the frontier ethos would not be so easily dislodged from the American spirit. It is like a trait from a distant forebear that keeps reappearing in the family tree. The effect of geography may be weakened through technology, but it cannot be eradicated entirely. And while it was geography that first brought us into a webwork of humanity by virtue of our exalted position vis-à-vis the other continents, it is technology that—rather than reversing this geographical trend—only intensifies it now, through our increasing immersion in the outside world. Again, we are *fated to lead.*

WE AMERICANS ARE QUASI-IMPERIALISTS, yet, as I've said, we have hated imperialism at the same time. The Oxford historian John Darwin writes that "American 'anti-imperialism' was rooted in the universal hostility of settler communities towards imperial authority and the fear of exploitation by merchants, bankers, shipowners and suppliers in the metropole." From the settlement of the thirteen colonies to the wagon trains headed to Oregon, European centers of power were held almost everywhere in suspicion: it was part of the pioneer mind-set. Still, by conquering the continent as we did, we found ourselves in an advantageous strategic situation, with stores of far-from-exhausted energy, besides, that required further outlets. In short, while denouncing empire, we soon found ourselves to have almost become one.

Darwin, in a pathbreaking 2008 book, *After Tamerlane: The Rise and Fall of Global Empires, 1400–2000,* notes that "empire is often seen as the original sin of European peoples, who corrupted an innocent world." Marxists, and later those on the academic Left, saw imperialism as almost literally the root of all political evil, and imperialism on college campuses today has been equated with sexism and racism: guilty of a similar magnitude of oppression and exploitation. But the truth, as Darwin goes on, is that empires have been with us since the dawn of antiquity and "lie in a process almost universal in human societies." The exchange of goods and ideas has always disrupted some societies more than others, "making them vulnerable to internal breakdown, and to takeover by outsiders." The disparities of military force between some societies and others have also played a role, so that empire, where different ethnic communities fall under the sway of a common ruler, "has been the default mode of political organization throughout most of history."[5] The capabilities needed to build strong states, owing to the patterns of geography, were simply not evenly distributed. Thus it was that most civilizational advancements occurred under imperial systems. The Golden Age of Islam was an imperial one, primarily under the Abbasids, and later in reduced measure under empires like the Fatimids and the Hafsids. The Mongols were cruel, but who did they subjugate or destroy? Other empires —the Khwarazmian, Bulgarian, Song, and so on. Before the European empires in Africa there were indigenous African empires of the Mali, Songhai, and others, complete with their own cultural achievements. The European empires, which the Left has in mind with its broadbrush condemnation of imperialism, came only after thousands of years of indigenous imperial rule in the Mediterranean, Persia, India, and China. In the early modern and modern eras, the multiethnic empires of the Habsburgs and Ottomans, with their tolerance and cosmopolitanism, protected minority rights better than did the uniethnic states that followed them. For millennia, in the interregnums between empires, anarchy often reigned. Who says imperialism is necessarily reactionary? Athens, Rome, Venice, and Great Britain were still, with all of their cruelties, the most enlightened regimes of their day.

To wit, the British may have ultimately failed in India, Palestine, and elsewhere, but the larger history of the British Empire is one of providing a vast armature of stability, fostered by sea and rail communications, where before there had been demonstrably less. In fact, as the Harvard historian Niall Ferguson has argued, the British Empire enabled a late-nineteenth- and early-twentieth-century form of globalization, before it was interrupted by a worldwide depression, two world wars, and a cold war. After that, a new form of globalization took root, made possible, as I have noted, by an American naval and air presence that has allowed for secure trade and energy transfers: that is, a free world trading system friendly to global manufacturing and investment. This American *system* is, Darwin points out, "imperial in all but name."[6] The building blocks of this American system were the Truman Doctrine, the Marshall Plan, the creation of the North Atlantic Treaty Organization (NATO), and the security pact with Japan, all put in place within six years after World War II, thereby securing Western Europe and East Asia against Soviet and Chinese communism. America had the economic means to do all this. After all, in 1945, the United States owned half the world's manufacturing capacity and was the only part of the industrialized world whose homeland had not been devastated by war.

Yale University historian Paul Kennedy writes that America has "faced the same tests and problems" as Rome, Britain, Ottoman Turkey, and other empires in the task of establishing a modicum of security in an anarchic world.[7] Of course, America, with its mission to establish a liberal world order, strives to be different from classic imperial systems. But even if it can succeed at that, a comparison with previous empires only helps our understanding of ourselves; we need to be clear-sighted about what we are and what role we are playing in the world. Indeed, the Cold War, which went on for forty-four years, continued the imperial tradition in the guise of an ideological struggle. Darwin calls this bipolar age "the other face of decolonization," whereby the collapse of British and French colonies forced the United States and the Soviet Union to compete for influence in the newly independent third world, enabling the building of two new empires.[8] These included full-fledged colonies in only a few cases, but they did feature a preponderance of American or Soviet influence. In fact, had the British and French empires not unraveled as they did in the late 1940s through the 1960s, the bipolar struggle between the United States and the Soviet Union might not have assumed such global dimensions, since it would have been reduced to a conflict over the fate of Central Europe alone.

In 1989, the Communist regimes in Central and Eastern Europe collapsed, followed by the disintegration of the Soviet Union itself in 1991. But while the United States is the last empire of sorts standing, with a gargantuan military for which there was no imaginable equal, it now has no possibility of bringing order to the world. To be clear: without America's current naval and air preponderance the world would be in an even more anarchic situation than it currently is. Yet it still does not follow that the total corpus of American power—military, economic, diplomatic, and geographic—is remotely capable of making the world a wholly pacific place. We can bring considerable order to the world, yet the distance between *considerable* order and *complete* order is vast. Therefore, what fills the gap between those two concepts must now be described. For the United States must henceforth deploy the resources of a continent in order to negotiate a global situation of comparative anarchy—one that has followed the imperial and postimperial Cold War ages.

IN THE FEBRUARY 1994 issue of *The Atlantic Monthly,* I published a cover story, "The Coming Anarchy," about how resource scarcity, demographic youth bulges, tribalism, sectarianism, crime, and disease were (and would be) fraying the social and political fabric of significant regions of the earth. I quoted a Canadian scholar, Thomas Homer-Dixon, describing a "stretch limo" world of wealthy countries and elites, concerned with technological refinements and financial markets, gazing out the window of their speeding vehicle at a poverty- and conflict-racked world where central authority was increasingly weak or nonexistent. Because this metaphorical stretch limo included not only specific countries but also the wealthy neighborhoods and luxury hotels of countries outside the stretch limo, it was possible for western elites to continue to deny this harsh reality beyond their own environs, even when they did venture abroad, from time to time, to the most materially benighted countries. Journalists might interview local civil society types, themselves educated in the West, and then declare hope for a given country, even as the writ of those local, western-educated elites ended beyond the capital city where semi-chaos reigned. The West African countries I used as examples in the first part of my long 1994 essay had all deteriorated further or collapsed outright by the end of the 1990s. Since then, those countries have survived as wards of western charities and security assistance programs, without in most cases building any substantial manufacturing bases with which they could have been lifted out of the danger zone. And while the rest of the world did not become like West Africa, it is clear that there are a significant number of countries, large and small, that have either disintegrated into chaos or partial chaos, or whose stability just cannot be taken for granted. Thus, the issues I raised almost a quarter century ago continue to resonate in America's quest for order in the world.

My argument was that rising populations, particularly in shantytowns on the outskirts of third world cities, in addition to resource scarcity—the depletion of water and nutrients in the soil, for example—did not *on their own* cause ethnic and sectarian strife, but did aggravate already existent communal divides. That led, in turn, to armed conflict in which the partitions between crime and war—both conventional and unconventional—were breaking down.

Yet, as we look around the world with which America must deal in the early twenty-first century and see a plethora of anarchic and quasi-anarchic situations, there are other background factors, very hard to admit, which must now be owned up to.

As we have seen, this is a postimperial world, with the Soviet empire gone and American power limited in its ability, for example, to set complex, populous, and faction-ridden Islamic societies to rights. Imperialism, though neither fair nor civil in many or most circumstances, did in fact provide much of Africa, Asia, and Latin America in the early modern and modern eras with minimum security and administrative order for significant periods of time. In the early modern and modern eras the Europeans divided the planet into a gridwork of entities, both artificial and not, and *governed.* Nevertheless, order did not break down upon the final demise of those European empires in the 1960s—in part because of the appearance of postimperial strongmen.

Because these new strongmen saw themselves as anti-western freedom fighters, they believed that they had the moral justification to govern as they pleased, and so they ruthlessly kept order within the same borders that the Europeans had, in many instances, created. And since these borders were often (though not always) artificial, cutting across sect and ethnic group, this generation of strongmen had to forge distinct national and, by inference, secular state identities in order to make their countries stable: such were the circumstances for the tyrannies of Hafez al-Assad, Saddam Hussein, Muammar Gaddafi, and others. Nevertheless, those postimperial strongmen, like the European colonialists before them, have lately been passing from the scene. And what did they leave in their wake?

A vacuum, it turns out.

In fact, those strongmen, particularly in the Middle East, had built no governing institutions to speak of. Instead, for decades they merely ran *moukhabarat* states—that is, states dominated by the secret police and other, related security services. So when the instruments of repression collapsed, there was little or no remaining bureaucratic framework to provide order, or even a semblance of civil society: all forms of organization between the regime at the top and the extended family and tribe at the bottom had long been obliterated. Thus, the state carried little meaning, and tribal and sectarian identities immediately helped fill the void. Those primordial identities were assisted by the latest technology in the form of social media, which, though they can help topple regimes, cannot provide a coherent and organized replacement pole of bureaucratic power to foster a new stability afterward. The very idea that following the age of postimperial strongmen would come an age of stable democracy as in Central and Eastern Europe after the Berlin Wall fell was naïve in the extreme. Unlike Central and Eastern Europe, societies in the Greater Middle East had comparatively less of a bourgeois tradition, with its raft of institutions, to rely upon.

What the United States has to contend with regarding the rise of the Islamic State and other jihadist movements, both Sunni and Shiite—as well as other, ethnically based risings from North Africa to India—is actually not altogether new in imperial and postimperial history. The seasoned Paris-based commentator William Pfaff, who covered international politics for decades before he died recently, observed that the rise of radical populist movements, demanding in many cases the restoration of a lost golden age, occurred twice in mid- and late-nineteenth-century Qing China (the Taiping and Boxer Rebellions), once in mid-nineteenth-century British India (the Sepoy Mutiny), and once in late-nineteenth-century British Sudan (the Mahdist Revolt). In this vein, as Pfaff explains so well, groups such as the Ugandan-based Lord's Resistance Army and the Nigerian-based Boko Haram, which we in the West label as merely "terrorist," are, in fact, redemptive millennial movements (as brutal as they are) that are a response to the twin threats of modernism and globalization.[9] In particular, the radical Islam raging across Africa represents the response of the communications revolution to failed societies: a generic Islamic extremism communicated by the media is the only answer to societal failure that many young African men can find.

And so we now have a Greater Islamic continuum between Europe and China that has undergone profound technological and social upheaval, even as creaky and calcified political structures, stemming from the period of European imperialism, have partially or completely disintegrated. Erupting out of this anarchy are violent and charismatic religious movements that declare war on the West, and particularly on the United States—that totemic symbol of the secular, modern world. The United States has responded by seeking to heal and stabilize the very places from where these jihadist warriors originate. But everything it tries has failed: whether President George W. Bush's full-bore nation-building in Iraq or President Barack Obama's more subtle, diplomatic, and special operations approach in Yemen. For the political and religious upheaval in the Islamic world is epic in scale and barely fathomable to outsiders, thus difficult, if not impossible, for the West to pivotally influence.

Indeed, the search for legitimacy, and for which path is the most just, has been going on in the House of Islam more or less since the collapse of the Ottoman Caliphate following World War I, and it shows no signs of abatement. A related problem is that while countries like Tunisia and Egypt within their current borders have a rich basis in history (Greater Carthage and the Nile Valley), and thus have relatively strong state identities, Libya, Syria, Iraq, and Yemen are but vague geographical expressions that, following the imperial and postimperial ages, have reverted to their default, ultrafragmented normal. (Of course, countries like Syria and Iraq also have a rich basis in ancient civilizations, but not in keeping with their official borders to the degree of Tunisia and Egypt.) In all or most of these places the Sunni regional hegemon, Saudi Arabia, and the Shiite regional hegemon, Iran, fight proxy wars. Afghanistan has been in a state of war for more than a third of a century. It is likely that the Levant, the Arabian Peninsula, and parts of North Africa will be in similar straits for a generation to come.

Alas, geopolitics—the battle for space and power—now occurs within states as well as between them. Cultural and religious differences are particularly inflamed, for as group differences melt down in the crucible of globalization, they have to be artificially reinvented in more blunt and ideological form by, as it turns out, the communications revolution. It isn't the clash of civilizations so much as the clash of artificially reconstructed civilizations that is taking place. Witness the Islamic State, which does not represent Islam per se, but Islam igniting with the tyrannical conformity and mass hysteria inspired by the Internet and social media. The postmodern reinvention of identities only hardens geopolitical divides.

Therefore, American power might be preponderant in relation to other powers, especially given the profound economic malaise in Europe, Russia, and China. But as the Middle East vividly demonstrates, preponderance does not equal control, or even much influence over geographical terrain from where warrior bands can plan attacks on the American homeland.

———

ASIA IS ANOTHER STORY.

Whereas the Greater Middle East is about the fragmentation of states and the proliferation of dirty, low-tech land insurgencies, Asia is about the hardening of states and the proliferation of high-tech naval, air, missile, and cyber weapons over a sterile and abstract maritime environment. Until relatively recently in history, Asian nations were focused internally, upon themselves. Vietnam and the Malay Peninsula were embroiled in Communist insurgencies and local wars. China was preoccupied with madcap Communist development schemes under Mao Zedong and later with capitalist-style regeneration under Deng Xiaoping and his successors. Meanwhile, Japan was somnolent under a regime of quasi-pacifism, an aftershock of its disastrous World War II militarism. But following the end of the Cold War, this situation began to evolve dramatically.

Sustained capitalist development in Asia has led not only to peace and harmony but to military acquisitions. By the 1990s, sustained double-digit economic growth was beginning to transform China into a major power with trading links and logistic tails throughout the globe. Therefore, for reasons of both status and self-interest, China embarked on an unprecedented military expansion akin to that of the United States at the turn of the twentieth century, after America's own breakneck post–Civil War economic growth. The unleashing of Chinese naval power has begun to erode America's unipolar military dominance of the Western Pacific. Japan, registering an existential threat to its security from this Chinese ex-

pansion, has shed its quasi-pacifism and is rediscovering nationalism, and thus preparing the groundwork for its own military
enlargement. Vietnam, Malaysia, and Singapore have followed suit,
purchasing submarines along with the latest arsenals of surface warships and air weaponry from both the West and Russia. The Philippines, meanwhile, after ejecting U.S. forces from Clark Air Base and
Subic Bay Naval Station in 1992, has been inviting back American
servicemen on a rotating basis, even as the two countries renew what
once had been one of America's most storied bilateral military alliances (though Manila's new government now puts this in doubt).
This all has to do with the growing threat from China, in which
Chinese naval assets—everything from fishing boats to coast guard
vessels to gray-hulled warships—are asserting claims to most of the
disputed waters of the South and East China Seas, where significant
hydrocarbon deposits and fish stocks are believed to be located.

China is, like the United States, both a nation and a continent
lying in the temperate latitudes, whose geography is well apportioned for global power projection, assuming it can assuage its
problems with ethnic minorities and reform its economy. The
South and East China Seas are blue-water extensions of this Chinese landmass, just as the Greater Caribbean is an extension of the
lower forty-eight states. And just as the United States was able to
use strategic control of the Greater Caribbean in order to dominate the Western Hemisphere, and thus affect the power balance
in the Eastern Hemisphere, China believes that its own eventual
domination of the South and East China Seas will unlock both the
larger Pacific and the Indian Ocean to its ever-expanding navy.
The narrow Strait of Malacca would serve, in this case, as the con-

duit to the Indian Ocean in the same way that the Panama Canal did for the Pacific. Remember that the Indian Ocean is the world's global energy interstate, across which tankers and container ships travel from the oil- and natural-gas-rich Arabian Peninsula and Iranian Plateau to the middle-class conurbations of East Asia. A substantial Chinese naval presence in the Western Pacific makes China a regional power—but a presence in *both* the Western Pacific and the Indian Ocean would make it a great power rival of the United States. Because the United States cannot tolerate a rival hegemon in the Eastern Hemisphere equivalent to itself in the Western Hemisphere, China's growing naval presence in the South and East China Seas must, therefore, be balanced against.

Whereas the crumbling states of the Middle East expose the limits of U.S. power, the more high-end and conventional Chinese maritime threat reveals the advantages of U.S. power. Projecting naval and air strength across oceanic distances is something no other state in history manages as well and effortlessly as the United States. The U.S. Navy and Air Force, while they will certainly have to make room for China's presence, nevertheless have it in their means to both avoid a war with China and yet prevent China from Finlandizing the countries of the South China Sea, even as Japan is defended.

America, I can never forget, looking out over San Diego Bay, is a Pacific country. It was Commodore Matthew Perry's four ships—the *Susquehanna, Mississippi, Plymouth,* and *Saratoga*—sailing into Tokyo Bay in 1853 that forcibly opened Japan to trade, helping along the collapse of the Tokugawa shogunate that led to the Meiji Restoration. America's first invasion of a large and populous country occurred in the Philippines in 1899, followed there by our first full-fledged nation-building experience. The Pacific, from Japan to the Solomon Islands, and including Burma and China, formed a principal theater of combat during World War II, with U.S. troops all over the South Seas. Then came the wars in Korea and Vietnam, whose troubled legacies are burned deep into the American historical consciousness. Today, there are many reasons for Washington to focus on the Asia-Pacific region. Asia, including India, is the geographical and demographic organizing principle of the world economy, containing the most important sea lines of communication, with major U.S. treaty allies in Japan, Korea, and the Philippines, and consequential de facto allies in Vietnam and Malaysia, all with teeming populations. This is to say nothing of our longstanding alliances with such countries as Thailand, Singapore, and Australia. As for China, its military rise arguably represents the single most important challenge to U.S. foreign policy in the early twenty-first century. The United States will deal with this challenge by, in part, utilizing India—a rising economic and military behemoth in its own right—as a hedge against China.

I am not describing a world necessarily on the brink of war, but a world that is more crowded, nervous, and anxious than perhaps at any moment in history, even as there remains no power as yet on the horizon with the imperial-like reach of the United States.

Making matters worse is not Chinese strength, but Chinese weakness. Though all of China's aggressive maritime activities have been in progress for a decade already, they are now increasingly occurring during a time of economic troubles at home. If those troubles become more acute, as they undoubtedly will, it will be hard to resist the urge to use Asian maritime disputes as a vehicle to stoke nationalism. For nationalism brings a measure of cohesion to societies threatening to fragment. Thus, the elegance in China's current form of aggression may wear off and be replaced by cruder, more impulsive actions. This process is insidious and may have already begun. The more active China is in its near abroad—in its adjacent seas, the Indian Ocean, and Central Asia—the more is at stake concerning its domestic economic turmoil.

THEN THERE IS EUROPE, which even after two world wars and a cold war lasting almost half a century still cries out for American help. Yes, the Cold War is over. But Russia is still big. It is also still an insecure land power that has suffered invasions not only from Hitler and Napoleon, but from Swedes, Lithuanians, and Poles and consequently requires a buffer zone of soft influence in Central and Eastern Europe. Thus, the new battleground will be the Intermarium, a term coined by the interwar Polish statesman and military leader Józef Piłsudski, which is Latin for "between the seas"—between the Baltic and Black Seas, that is. From the Baltic states and Poland in the north, down through the Balkans and eastward across the Black Sea to the Caucasus, there is a belt of countries—the Greater Intermarium, I call it—that will be contested between Russia and the West.

Instead of ground troops, the new face of Russian imperialism consists of intelligence operations, subversion, pipeline routes, and corruption. Now and in the future, the United States will lead the NATO response: employing a suite of assets from information operations to cyberattacks to economic sanctions against Russia. Why must the United States do this? Why can't, for example, Germany be the leader? Because the United States is not a normal country: its geographic bounty gave it the possibility of becoming a world power, and with that power it has developed long-standing obligations, which, on account of its continued economic and social dynamism relative to other powers, it keeps. Meanwhile, Germany famously remains—as it has been since the late nineteenth century—too big for Europe and too small for the world. However benign it may appear and may desire to be, Germany must itself, over the long haul, be somewhat restrained by U.S. power and also by the European Union.

All this occurs while the social welfare model of European economies is generally no longer sustainable, and Europe's politicians find it hard to gather the will to decisively fix the problem. Europeans want freedom but they do not want to make sufficient sacrifices for the sake of it (such as restructuring their social welfare states), even as European elites have long ago abandoned traditional nationalism. The consequence of their abandonment of nationalism is the rise of feverish populist movements in many a European capital, supported by socially and economically marginal elements of the population, thus putting the future of the European Union itself at risk. The low defense budgets—only a handful of countries reach the NATO guideline of 2 percent of GDP—are a consequence of such demoralized populations. This is the new and subtle postmodern face of surrender.

Europe prospered during a decades-long interregnum following World War II when it was cut off from both the Arab world and Russia. But now with the collapse of Arab police states and the rise of Russian revisionism, Europe is dissolving into a fluid classical geography, uniting it with Afro-Eurasia. The millions of Muslim migrants from the chaos in North Africa and the Levant—as well as Russia's intervention in Ukraine and its threats to the Baltic states—tell the story.

As for Russia, beyond the rule of the neoczarist Vladimir Putin lies, perhaps, true liberalization—but much more likely either partial disintegration or even more extreme tyranny. Russia is bureaucratically and organizationally weak, except, of course, for its military and security services. The 1990s were a decade of social chaos, and since then Putin has ruled through a camarilla of oligarchs rather than through impersonal institutions. So Russia remains an immense landmass, covering half the longitudes of the earth, on the brink of anarchy, staved off in turn by autocracy. It could be a future Yugoslavia lite.

So far we have seen the weakening and collapse of small and medium-sized states in Africa and the Middle East. But quasi-anarchy in larger states like Russia and China, on which the territorial organization of Eurasia hinges, could be next—tied to structural economic causes linked, in turn, to slow growth worldwide.

We are dealing here with forces too large for the United States to control, even as it is the United States alone that has the power to pivotally influence events for the good. Especially as Europe grows weaker and is geographically reintegrated into a maelstrom of Afro-Eurasian history, pounded both from within and without, the United States becomes the bastion of the West.

As for Latin America and Africa, the former for reasons of both geography and economics is a region where U.S. influence is historically rooted and undeniable, while the latter, because of weak states, the risk of global disease pandemics, and the rise of nascent and restive middle classes, is a place that simply cannot be ignored either. For example, witness the Greater Gulf of Guinea, from Mauritania to Namibia: a world of weak or failing states, Islamic terrorism, narcotics traffic, money laundering, rampant disease, endemic piracy, immense energy deposits, and occasional conflicts.

But the fact is, no place in the world can be ignored. That is the legacy of America's geography, intensified by modern history and postmodern technology. And because geopolitics is now being played out against a setting of globalization, every crisis interacts in some way with every other one: the world is increasingly claustrophobic. If the United States concedes too much to China in the South China Sea, for example, it affects America's reputation for power in Europe and the Middle East—to say nothing about its reputation for power in the Indian subcontinent and northeast Asia. But through it all, because of the size and power of its own geography, the American electorate—as I've seen in my journey— only intermittently registers this outer world in upheaval. Despite technology, many of us feel removed from things.

OVER THE HORIZON, BEYOND THE LINE of gray-hulled ships, on the other side of the Pacific lies a world in the Eastern Hemisphere where war and conflict are assuming the futuristic outlines governed by robotics, cyber capabilities, and precision-guided weaponry unimaginable just a few decades ago: indeed, air and sea warfare require immense stores of capital as well as substantial scientific and technological bases. But beyond Asia itself, in the Greater Middle East, lies the world of the *Iliad,* where just one gun—or one executioner's knife and a video camera—buys you entry into the battlespace. Obviously, the worlds of Star Wars and of Greek antiquity often merge, and air and cyber power can be useful against the challenge of ancient warriors. But clearly, in an era of global conflict that is both antique and postmodern, there have been and will be things that we Americans do well and cannot do well, things that we can do and cannot—that is, should not—do.

And yet, we now have in the American capital of Washington, D.C., and the larger East Coast an imperial class that sometimes wants to do nearly everything.

What is an imperial class, and what are its beliefs?

An imperial class is a large group of people that has a deeply evolved sense of mission and whose professional interests are connected to that mission succeeding. They number journalists as well as policy experts at think tanks who collectively define the debate among elites throughout the Boston–New York–Washington media corridor and by defining that debate help determine the opinions that bombard any White House on the foreign policy front. This class is financially well off and generally educated at the best schools. It is the product of decades of prosperity going back to the post–World War II years. Whereas Washington in the mid-twentieth century had barely a handful of think tanks, the city is now jam-packed with them. As for the media, it now constitutes a power center all its own and is dominated by both liberal internationalists and neoconservative interventionists, each of whom have in the past supported using the American military to impose American values.[10] They label those values *universal,* but that is how many imperial classes—from the Romans onward—labeled their own beliefs. When Commodore Perry arrived in Tokyo Bay in 1853 he believed he was bringing Christianity and commerce to the heathens. The same when Protestant missionaries set out from New England and the Midwest in the mid-nineteenth century to proselytize in China and Greater Syria. First it was Christianity that they thought they were bringing, but when the locals proved unreceptive to that message, the mission changed to bringing education, and finally to human rights. It was all part of an imperial mind-set that sought to *civilize.* That is why imperialism and the missionary impulse go hand in hand.

None of this is a conspiracy, nor by any stretch is it necessarily illiberal or even in many cases militaristic. Indeed, a significant section of this imperial class can be defined as humanitarians, who believe America's proper role in the world is to prevent genocide and otherwise protect embattled ethnic, religious, and sectarian minorities: i.e., to export human rights. Imperialism, keep in mind, can be described as a relatively weak form of sovereignty exercised by a great power. It is weak because the imperial authority does not control far-flung regions to the degree that it controls its own homeland, and yet it can still affect outcomes and processes to a reasonable extent in various parts of the globe. Thus, a humanitarianism that seeks to affect outcomes overseas may fall well within the rubric of imperialism, whereas isolationism and neo-isolationism usually do not.

Perhaps the best example of imperialism explained as humanitarianism is Rudyard Kipling's 1899 poem "The White Man's Burden," which to our contemporary ears certainly sounds racist but was arguably a somewhat idealistic work of literature, because it sought to convey the responsibility that richer and more-developed countries had to poorer and less-developed ones. Actually, Kipling wrote the poem to encourage what he saw as America's so-called civilizing mission in the Philippines.

Fast-forward to the 1990s. America was at peace, a unipolar power, with no other rival to threaten it, basking in its victory in the Cold War. Energy markets were stable. There was no obvious national interest to intervene anywhere. The 9/11 attacks still lay in the future, and the expansion of the Chinese navy was only just beginning. Yet America did intervene with military force—in Somalia, Haiti, Bosnia, and Kosovo. The pressure for such interventions came from the imperial class. One could easily argue that at least in some of those cases military intervention was the right thing to do. My point is not that the interventions were wrong, but that they happened. And they happened repeatedly, without an obvious and overwhelming national interest. One might assume that the more secure an imperial power is, the less likely it is to intervene anywhere. But the 1990s showed this not to be the case. Only the memory of interventions gone awry, or an end to economic prosperity that in turn leads to a sharp decline in military budgets and a drawdown of both the power and number of elites, can seriously undermine the imperial instinct.

To emphasize, my point is not to condemn the imperial class but merely to register that it exists and can be defined as such.

Bear in mind that conquest is itself a source of weakness (a conviction held by both George Kennan and Edward Gibbon), since the moment you intervene with a heavy hand and remain for any length of time in a far-off place, you take moral and political responsibility for its governance, thereby heaping new burdens upon yourself.[11] The Soviet Union collapsed partly because of the burden of supporting Communist regimes in Central and Eastern Europe; the United States has remained prosperous because its heavy-handed imperial adventures, in places like the Philippines, Vietnam, and Iraq, have been relatively rare. Concomitantly, military intervention can be a sign of isolationism, since it implies a long-standing neglect of the far-off land in question until you impulsively dispatch troops there. This is a common pattern, especially in the media, which ignores many a crucial place for years on end, until they suddenly discover it one day in a feverish news cycle and demand action *now.*

THE "UNIVERSALISM" OF THE IMPERIAL CLASS is countered by the "particularism" of traditional realists. Universalism applies the same principles everywhere, since such principles are self-evidently American, and therefore moral. Universalism downplays "national peculiarities," which can be so bewildering to Americans, and therefore relieves Americans of the burden of *dealing with the world as it is.* Particularism accepts the world as it is, with all of its cultural and ideological differences; it favors working with allies and getting them to do as much of the work as possible in an economy-of-force approach; it is wary of entanglements that bog you down in one place.[12] Barring an economic collapse or a demonstrably failed military intervention, it is often only this particularism that stands in the way of imperialist universalism, however justified that universalism may be on certain occasions.

Particularism, the American diplomat George F. Kennan intimated, has been assisted by continentalism. Continentalism means a focus on the continental United States, with its plethora of internal problems and challenges and staggering richness of geography and history. This focus on America's own affairs often tempers one's obsession with the need to solve the outside world's problems. Of course, DeVoto's genius was to see that there have been and will be those moments when even the most ardent continentalism must, nevertheless, give way to responsibilities abroad. It is a matter of balance and discernment.

WHAT DO BALANCE AND DISCERNMENT look like on a daily basis?

To explain, back to DeVoto.

In *The Course of Empire,* DeVoto discusses how in the contest between the British and the Americans for the Rocky Mountains and Pacific Northwest, both sides sought to make alliances with as many Indian tribes as they could, while buying the neutrality of others. Here in a key paragraph DeVoto sketches the American strategy for conquering its new empire west of the Mississippi and Missouri Rivers:

> The military actions in the west were microscopic and exceedingly important. They were not decisive in American

survival but the very nature of American nationalism turned on them. So did the area of the American empire; so did the greatest national wealth the United States was to have. Here was an action in delicate equipoises, constantly oscillating. Extemporized organizations of frontiersmen, ranging across great distances and seldom acting for very long at a time, provided just enough weight to turn and keep the balance American.[13]

In describing the immense tracts of the American West that were won essentially, at least at first, by scattered groups of frontiersmen (before the U.S. Army entered with campaigns whose formations and tactics were irregular more than conventional), DeVoto is, of course, without being aware of it, foreseeing the actions of American special operations forces around the world today. Indeed, allowing for the advance of communications technology, the far-flung outposts of a chaotic and postimperial world are now as distant from one another as those of the nineteenth-century trans-Mississippi West, from the Great Plains to the Pacific, with its mobile Indian guerrillas. The United States can project power over great distances through its navy and air force, but it cannot occupy or administer large or even small patches of ground for any length of time, so it uses its equivalent of frontiersmen—special operations forces—to ally with some factions, buy the neutrality of others, and in general solve problems early on, when it is possible. Of course, that is still unsatisfactory. But it is the best that can be done under the circumstances. This is not isolationism, which would have nothing to do with these chaotic outposts, but neither is it full-fledged imperialism, which would seek to administer these territories on some level—and change their societies into what we are.

As the military historian Andrew J. Birtle writes, "The U.S. Army was in many ways the child of the frontier. . . . Overworked, underfunded, and dispersed among many small posts," the army struggled to enforce the rule of law and treaties and "regulate Indian-white contact." Birtle goes on: "Rather than abandoning traditional methods of warfare for Indian ways," the army "blended the strong points of each," with Indian war-fighting and raiding methods taught at West Point from 1835 onward.[14]

My point is not at all to justify how the army treated the Indians; it is only to say that the decades of contact and warfare between the two sides had immense influence on the army's culture and doctrine. To be sure, as the military historian Brian McAllister Linn notes, while depicting the horrors inflicted on the Indians by U.S. soldiers during the Seminole wars, "frontier warfare brought out some of the worst characteristics of the Heroic martial tradition."[15]

The Indian Wars were about conquest. While some of the techniques deriving from those wars have their echoes in the counterinsurgency doctrine of today—which emphasizes small mobile units working with indigenous populations—conquest will only bring twenty-first-century America to grief: Iraq was an example of the frontier tradition having gone too far. I feel this deeply at a personal level, having supported the war, and having tried in my analyses to learn from it ever since.

But don't assume that a catastrophe like Iraq cannot happen

again. For the impulse to repeat the mistakes of Iraq is still there among the imperial class. Witness the catcalls of "appeasement" every time an administration acts insufficiently aggressive—at least according to some in New York and Washington. Yet we need to realize that every adversary is not Hitler, and even getting Hitler right in the 1930s was not as clear-cut as it now seems, given that 16 million troops and civilians had been killed only twenty years earlier in World War I and no one wanted to repeat that mistake. Appeasement in some degree—historically a common technique of policy—will be a part of any responsible president's future. Using it as a *gotcha* will not work. Fate is not that knowable in advance. Grand strategy is about marrying ends to means, about doing what you can, consistent with the nation's capabilities and resources. That means not fighting every battle. It means, for instance, a light and subtle footprint in the Greater Middle East, and perhaps a slightly heavier one in Europe and East Asia.

THE LATE WILLIAM PFAFF, in a withering critique of U.S. foreign policy, *The Irony of Manifest Destiny,* has several wise and perceptive insights pertinent to this discussion. He writes that Woodrow Wilson reinvented Manifest Destiny "as a divinely ordained mission to humanity," and furthermore, "the juxtaposition of global threat and Wilsonian world reform seems the only way the American national imagination has found to deal with the anxieties and fears produced by the loss of that geographical isolation." In other words, no longer protected by two oceans, making the rest of the world just like ourselves is the only way Americans can find to deal

with their new vulnerability; in this way democracy promotion becomes "a virtual form of isolationism." Indeed, for Americans, it is
always about their own historical experience, never about those of
others, even when they focus on other countries. After all, Progress
is inevitable in the Western mind, and particularly in the American one, which believes history moves toward an intelligible conclusion.[16]

But Progress, sad to say, is not inevitable. American exceptionalism, the belief that we are a unique people with a unique mission
in history, may arguably be true, but even if it is true, believing it
too intensely can lead to disaster. Here is Melville on Captain Ahab
and his crew: "Ah! how they still strove through that infinite blue-
ness to seek out the thing that might destroy them!"[17]

Who are we?

The late American poet and literary critic Charles Olson said,
"We are the last 'first' people": the last primitive people, that is, to
conquer *space,* with the will to "overcome" nature at the bottom of
our souls. The first real *space* we conquered was the Great Plains,
"the fulcrum of America," Olson writes. Then it was the Pacific,
presaged in the Great Plains—a metaphor for the world.[18] And what
form does that conquest take now? It takes the form of trying to
export our civic religion: representative democracy, human rights,
rule of law, and so forth. But this assumes that no history anywhere
matters except our own. It assumes that the very different historical
experiences of other peoples around the globe and the conclusions
that they draw from them do not count. While democracy, human
rights, and the rest are self-evidently good, that does not mean
other peoples will arrive at them—or even at variations of them—

through the processes we demand. And this is to say nothing of the fact that such tenets as democracy and human rights are themselves not always in harmony: for in a number of places, minority rights are better protected by monarchies and dictatorships than by tyrannies of the majority or by outright chaos—which ill-conceived experiments in democracy periodically bring about.

We should remember over and over again that the frontier was ultimately about practicality—about doing rather than imagining and living according to an applied wisdom of common sense. Nobody embodied that sensibility as much as the great twentieth-century American diplomat George Kennan, born and raised in the heartland state of Wisconsin. Kennan believed in things that would horrify sectors of today's policy elite. For example, he thought that the domestic character of a state was less important than its international behavior, even if its government acted repressively internally: if it was responsible abroad and its foreign policy served our purposes, that was enough. He thought that the maintenance of the balance of power was more important than a proclamation of moral principles. Kennan was less of an original thinker than a reminder and scold of what the Founding Fathers had stood for in international relations. As his biographer, Yale professor John Lewis Gaddis, explains, Kennan believed that the security of the United States was less endangered by its adversaries than by the illusions of its own leaders and elites.[19]

I LOOK OUT AT THESE gray-hulled ships bound for Cathay: the Cathay to which the modernist poet Hart Crane alluded, now signifying our immersion in the wider world with its infinite webwork of problems and possibilities. Columbus may have (at first) misidentified America as Cathay. But Cathay, nevertheless, has meaning as America's ultimate destiny. These gray-hulls defend a liberal maritime order, something that is the greatest single good any nation provides the world in the early twenty-first century, something that none of America's detractors can credibly deny or take away—no matter our periodic blunders. We cannot willingly fade away—not without a successor on the horizon that roughly approximates our own values. Great Britain at the end of World War II had us to rely on, so it could disband its empire without catastrophe for civilization: it could *appease* American power, in other words. But now we have nobody in sight. The Asia-Pacific region, as a stable balance of power regime, just does not work without the U.S. Navy. The Middle East probably will not fix itself, for it has yet to find an adequate answer to the collapse of the Ottoman Empire a hundred years ago. Europe's post–World War II order, built on a common economic union, has been weakening and is therefore unequal to the task of confronting on its own an unstable and assertive Russia. Thus, we must sustain ourselves internationally, even if we cannot solve many a problem and must avoid costly interventions, even as we remember that the lessons of successful empires have been restraint, caution, and strategic patience.

Because our geography works to a degree that the geographies of other continents do not, we as a people are freighted with responsibilities, both moral and amoral. Which means that we must go back to the idea of what the frontier really represented in the eighteenth and nineteenth centuries. The frontier was about being frugal with our assets. It was about pushing out over the boundary line, but only while tending to our own. It was about maintaining supply lines, however much that slowed us up. It was about reaching but not overreaching, even as it was about not being timid. And so above all it was about pragmatism.

We must keep the mind-set of the frontier in the present tense. The frontier has been the secret sauce behind American exceptionalism, which is in strong measure the gift of geography.

Do not ever take these ships for granted. Remember that Athens, whose democratic empire spawned such great works of philosophy and literature, was synonymous with maritime power. Looking out at the San Diego harbor, I think of the gift of American geography that I have seen firsthand, as though it were the arcing span of a colossal bridge: forest, prairie, desert, and mountains all cohering into a unit that commands a human dimension. These ships are here in these berths not only because of our sheer ambition and missionary tendency as a nation, but because of our boisterous vitality: the American public, with all of its complaints and disappointments and trysts with populist demagogues, in the end trusts and accepts its governing elite on matters of critical concern abroad. Yet these ships may not be endangered only by foreign navies, Chinese or otherwise. They are also just as likely to be endangered by catastrophes of our own making that sunder that trust. And so these ships will be here in these berths only as long as we remember all and not just some of the lessons of the frontier.

EPILOGUE

Technology has not negated geography. It has only made geography smaller and more claustrophobic, so that each patch of earth is more dearly held and more closely contested than ever before, while each region and crisis zone is more interconnected with every other one as never before. My father's Lower 48 was incomparably vaster than the one through which I have passed, and incomparably more isolated from Europe and Asia, though the cataclysm of World War II brought our troops overseas in any case.

Bernard DeVoto wrote about how we filled up a continent. Given the spread of cities and suburbs and exurbs, and restrictions on growth in a water-starved age, the continent is now filled up and starting to dissolve into an increasingly smaller world. This dissolution, because it happens unevenly—because it affects different parts of the population differently—only aggravates our internal divisions. The sharp and well-defined features of the giant, that being the United States, are beginning to slacken.

The roads and highways of America, with their energizing early morning talk at gas station convenience stores—alongside the array of chewing tobaccos and exotic coffee machines—represent a unified culture. But that is only one social aspect of the country: for wherever you are, you must always be conscious of other realities that contradict the one before your eyes. And even within that unified culture, people's silences about politics are unsettling, given that their speech is alive with life's daily problems. This suggests alienation, making people prone to demagogues in more difficult times. I think of our inhospitable desert reaches, which make for only a flimsy civilizational hold: we are not as secure—or as mature—a society as we think, even as we remain more powerful than any competitor.

Meanwhile, our expanding urban areas are becoming global city-states, with increasingly dense and meaningful connections with the outside world. But the weakness of global culture is that, having psychologically disconnected itself from any specific homeland, it has no terrain to defend or to fight for, and therefore no anchoring beliefs beyond the latest fashion or media craze. So we unravel into the world. And the more disconnected we become from our territorial roots—the more urbanized and globalized we become—the greater the danger of artificially reconstructing American identity in more severe and ideological form, so that we risk radicalization at home. We are not safe, in other words, from all the demons of history that have beset Europe and Asia, especially as we integrate more and more with other parts of the globe.

I think of the Illinois cornfields, rich beyond imagining, that ultimately allow elites in Washington to contemplate *action*. But then I think of the lava-scarred, cindery deserts of Greater Utah. The Great Plains and the thinly soiled Rocky Mountain West were the great discontinuity in our history, making communalism a necessity and exposing the individualism of American myth as partially false. The communalism that successfully allowed for the completion of Manifest Destiny now has a complement in multilateralism abroad. The more immersed we become in the wider world with all of its problems, the less able we will be to go it alone. For just as isolationism makes increasingly less sense as the world gets smaller, unilateralism makes less sense as every crisis is entangled with every other. Our first empire was built on both individualism and communalism: our foreign policy must be likewise.

Through multilateralism we will minimize the risks of our military deployments abroad. We must also be careful to identify ourselves with the masses of the former third world, Islamic and otherwise, as these same masses remove themselves from the village, throng to the half-completed city and shantytown, and in their migrating billions determine the future of humanity perhaps to a degree greater than anyone in the West. Only by avoiding self-inflicted catastrophes and joining spiritually with other peoples and nations can we keep the home front at peace with itself.

The answer to the devastation of Wheeling, West Virginia, and Portsmouth, Ohio, is not retrenchment or isolationism. Our obligations abroad are profound, and if we deny them we will only bring havoc upon ourselves, as new forms of terrorism and totalitarianism unhinge the global economic system. Precisely because of our relative continental isolation, our allies are not close but on the frontier, on the Rimland of Eurasia, in close proximity to the great autocratic powers of that supercontinent. In defending them, we defend a liberal world order. But also precisely because of Wheeling and Portsmouth and the challenges they represent, we must keep from getting bogged down anywhere, except at home. For the shrinkage and crowding of the globe means a world of never-ending, rapid-fire crises, so that quagmire carries greater costs than ever before. We must imagine ourselves forever on the hundredth meridian of longitude in Nebraska, where the landscape features sharpen and minimalize in the increasingly thinning air. The water table underneath continues to diminish as we head west. The margin for error narrows.

ACKNOWLEDGMENTS

Anna Pitoniak at Random House made the manuscript immeasurably better by means of a light but deft editorial touch, combined with key suggestions for drawing out the main points. Henry Thayer at Brandt & Hochman Literary Agents was the first reader to whom I showed this manuscript. He subsequently had sharp insights about how to take it to a higher level. William Whitworth, the editor of *The Atlantic* between 1981 and 1999, provided his usual wise counsel and encouragement, especially on grammar. Once again, I thank the late Carl D. Brandt for encouraging me to pursue this project as well as others. Indeed, Carl's love for the American West was unmatched. Critical support also came from literary agents Gail Hochman and Marianne Merola, and from Kate Medina at Random House.

An early section of Chapter III ran as an essay in *The Atlantic* in

March 2000, under the title "What Makes History: The Lessons of a New England Landscape." I am grateful to Bill Whitworth for acquiring it, Cullen Murphy for editing it, and the late Michael Kelly for publishing it. *The Atlantic, The National Interest,* and Stratfor also published much smaller sections of Chapter V, for which I am grateful to James Bennet, Scott Stossel, Kate Julian, Jacob Heilbrunn, and David Judson. Regarding the concept of "vertical" and "horizontal" landscapes, in reference to the eastern and western halves of the United States, I was inspired by William Least Heat-Moon's magnificent Proustian study of one county in Kansas, *PrairyErth,* published by Houghton Mifflin in 1991.

I could not have undertaken this project without the support of the Center for a New American Security in Washington, and the intellectual freedom that it truly encourages, for which I thank CEO Michèle Flournoy, President Richard Fontaine, and Director of Studies Shawn Brimley.

I thank my assistant, Elizabeth M. Lockyer, with help from Dede and Marc Rathbun, for their continued professional services on my behalf, and my wife, Maria Cabral, for her love and support.

SOME WORKS RELEVANT
TO THE TEXT

Birtle, Andrew J. *U.S. Army Counterinsurgency and Contingency Operations Doctrine 1860–1941.* Washington, D.C.: Center of Military History, United States Army, 2004.

Boorstin, Daniel J. *Hidden History: Exploring Our Secret Past.* New York: Harper & Row, 1987.

Bowen, Catherine Drinker, Mirrielees, Edith R., Schlesinger, Arthur M., Jr., and Stegner, Wallace. *Four Portraits and One Subject: Bernard DeVoto.* Boston: Houghton Mifflin, 1963.

Cowley, Malcolm. *The Portable Faulkner.* New York: Viking Press, 1946.

Crane, Hart. *The Bridge.* Paris: Black Sun Press, 1930.

Darwin, John. *After Tamerlane: The Rise and Fall of Global Empires, 1400–2000.* New York: Bloomsbury Press, 2008.

DeVoto, Bernard. *Mark Twain's America.* 1932. Reprinted with an introduction by Louis J. Budd. Lincoln, Nebraska: University of Nebraska Press, 1997.

———. *The Year of Decision: 1846.* 1942. Reprinted with a foreword by Arthur M. Schlesinger, Jr. Boston: Houghton Mifflin, 1989.

———. *Across the Wide Missouri.* Boston: Houghton Mifflin, 1947.

———. *The Course of Empire.* Boston: Houghton Mifflin, 1952.

Donald, David Herbert. *Lincoln.* New York: Simon & Schuster, 1995.

Frost, Robert. "The Gift Outright." *Virginia Quarterly Review,* Spring 1942.

Gaddis, John Lewis. *George F. Kennan: An American Life.* New York: Penguin Press, 2011.

Hammer, Langdon. *Hart Crane and Allen Tate: Janus-Faced Modernism.* Princeton, NJ: Princeton University Press, 1993.

Kaplan, Robert D. *An Empire Wilderness: Travels into America's Future.* New York: Random House, 1998.

———. *The Revenge of Geography: What the Map Tells Us About Coming Conflicts and the Battle Against Fate.* New York: Random House, 2012.

———. "Homage to the Lower 48." Austin, TX: Stratfor, July 10, 2013.

Kennedy, Paul. *Grand Strategies in War and Peace.* New Haven, CT: Yale University Press, 1991.

Krakauer, Jon. *Under the Banner of Heaven: A Story of Violent Faith.* New York: Doubleday, 2003.

Least Heat-Moon, William. *PrairyErth.* Boston: Houghton Mifflin, 1991.

Linn, Brian McAllister. *The Echo of Battle: The Army's Way of War.* Cambridge, MA: Harvard University Press, 2007.

McPhee, John. *Basin and Range.* New York: Farrar, Straus and Giroux, 1981.

Mead, Walter Russell. "The Jacksonian Tradition." *The National Interest,* Winter 1999–2000.

Merry, Robert W. *A Country of Vast Designs: James K. Polk, the Mexican War and the Conquest of the American Continent.* New York: Simon & Schuster, 2009.

Morris, Edmund. *The Rise of Theodore Roosevelt.* New York: Random House, 1979.

Nash, Roderick Frazier. *Wilderness and the American Mind.* 1967. New Haven, CT: Yale University Press, 1982.

Olson, Charles. *Call Me Ishmael.* San Francisco: City Lights Books, 1947.

Pfaff, William. *The Irony of Manifest Destiny: The Tragedy of America's Foreign Policy.* New York: Walker & Company, 2010.

Reynolds, David S. *Walt Whitman's America: A Cultural Biography.* New York: Knopf, 1995.

Stegner, Wallace. *Beyond the Hundredth Meridian: John Wesley Powell and the Second Opening of the West.* Boston: Houghton Mifflin, 1954.

————. *The Gathering of Zion: The Story of the Mormon Trail.* New York: McGraw-Hill, 1964.

————. *The Uneasy Chair: A Biography of Bernard DeVoto.* Garden City, NY: Doubleday, 1974.

Stratfor. "The Geopolitics of the United States, Part 1: The Inevitable Empire," August 24, 2011.

Toker, Franklin. *Pittsburgh: A New Portrait.* 1989. Pittsburgh, PA: University of Pittsburgh Press, 2009.

Webb, Walter Prescott. *The Great Plains.* 1931. Lincoln: University of Nebraska Press, 1981.

Whitman, Walt. "Song of the Open Road," 1856.

Williams, William Carlos. *Paterson.* 1946–58. New York: New Directions, 1963.

Wilmerding, John. *American Light: The Luminist Movement, 1850–1875.* Princeton, NJ: Princeton University Press, 1989.

Winchester, Simon. *The Men Who United the States: America's Explorers, Inventors, Eccentrics, and Mavericks, and the Creation of One Nation, Indivisible.* New York: HarperCollins, 2013.

NOTES

INVOCATION

1. William Carlos Williams, *Paterson* (New York: New Directions, 1963), preface, 3.

CHAPTER II: A CONTINENTAL EMPIRE

1. Bernard DeVoto, *The Year of Decision: 1846* (Boston: Houghton Mifflin, 1989), 67.
2. Wallace Stegner, *The Uneasy Chair: A Biography of Bernard DeVoto* (Garden City, NY: Doubleday, 1974), 222–23.
3. Ibid., 232.
4. DeVoto, *The Year of Decision,* xiv and 208–9.
5. Catherine Drinker Bowen, Edith R. Mirrielees, Arthur M. Schlesinger, Jr., and Wallace Stegner, *Four Portraits and One Subject: Bernard DeVoto* (Boston: Houghton Mifflin, 1963), 4.
6. Ibid., 23.

7. DeVoto, *Year of Decision,* xii. Bowen, Mirrielees, Schlesinger, and Stegner, *Four Portraits and One Subject,* 57–60.

8. Ibid.

9. Stegner, *The Uneasy Chair,* 224–27.

10. DeVoto, *Year of Decision,* xi–xii. Stegner, *The Uneasy Chair,* 224–27. Bowen, Mirrielees, Schlesinger, and Stegner, *Four Portraits and One Subject,* 57–60.

11. Stephen E. Ambrose, introduction to *Year of Decision,* 2000.

12. DeVoto, *Year of Decision,* invocation.

13. Ibid., 7–8.

14. Ibid.

15. Ibid., 137–39.

16. Ibid., 54.

17. Ibid., 82–83, 97, 165, and 466.

18. Ibid., 115, 118–19, 176–78, 249–50, and 302–5.

19. Wallace Stegner, *Beyond the Hundredth Meridian: John Wesley Powell and the Second Opening of the West* (Boston: Houghton Mifflin, 1954), 256–57.

20. DeVoto, *Year of Decision,* 497.

21. Ibid., 495–96 and 498.

22. Bernard DeVoto, *Across the Wide Missouri* (Boston: Houghton Mifflin, 1947), 3, 5, and 61.

23. Ibid., 15–16.

24. Ibid., 140.

25. Ibid., 300–301.

26. Ibid., 245–46.

27. Bernard DeVoto, *The Course of Empire* (Boston: Houghton Mifflin, 1952), xxxi, 60, and 228.

28. Ibid., 406–7.

29. Bernard DeVoto, *Mark Twain's America,* introduction by Louis J. Budd (Lincoln, Nebraska: University of Nebraska Press, 1997), ix–x.

30. William Carlos Williams, *Paterson* (New York: New Directions, 1963), 28.

31. Dwight Macdonald, "To the White House," *New York Review of Books,* February 1, 1963.

32. DeVoto, *Mark Twain's America,* 48, 51, 54, and 105–6.

33. Ibid.

CHAPTER III: NOTES ON A VERTICAL LANDSCAPE

1. Daniel J. Boorstin, *The Americans: The Colonial Experience* (New York: Random House, 1958), chapter 24.

2. Robert D. Kaplan, "What Makes History: The Lessons of a New England Landscape," *The Atlantic,* March 2000.

3. Edmund Morris, *The Rise of Theodore Roosevelt* (New York: Random House, 1979), 377 and 473.

4. Franklin Toker, *Pittsburgh: A New Portrait* (Pittsburgh: University of Pittsburgh Press, 2009).

5. Adam Wren, "Iran? Is That the One We Invaded?" *Politico,* July 16, 2015.

CHAPTER IV: NOTES ON A HORIZONTAL LANDSCAPE

1. Wallace Stegner, *The Gathering of Zion: The Story of the Mormon Trail* (New York: McGraw-Hill, 1964), 1–2, 4, and 111 of University of Nebraska Press edition.

2. Ibid., 4–7, 122, and 153–54.

3. Walter Prescott Webb, *The Great Plains* (Lincoln: University of Nebraska Press, 1981), 17 and 21–25.

4. Ibid., 43–44 and 52.

5. Ibid., 140–41, 184–85, and 201.

6. Ibid., 207–8, 226, and 245–46.

7. Ibid., 486, 489, 491, 507, and 513.

8. Wallace Stegner, *Beyond the Hundredth Meridian: John Wesley Powell and the Second Opening of the West* (Boston: Houghton Mifflin, 1954), 3.

9. Ibid., 17, 39, 42–43, 62, and 72.

10. Ibid., 93 and 110–11.

11. Ibid., 113 and 122.

12. Ibid., 230–31, 308, and 353.

13. Ibid., 174.

14. Simon Schama, *Landscape and Memory* (New York: Knopf, 1995), 394–95 and 397.

15. Robert Frost, "The Gift Outright," *Virginia Quarterly Review,* Spring 1942.

16. David S. Reynolds, *Walt Whitman's America: A Cultural Biography* (New York: Knopf, 1995), 298.

17. Xilao Li, "Walt Whitman and Asian American Writers," *Walt Whitman Quarterly Review,* 10, no. 4 (1993).

CHAPTER V: CATHAY

1. John R. Hale, *Lords of the Sea: The Epic Story of the Athenian Navy and the Birth of Democracy* (New York: Viking Penguin, 2009), xxiii–xxv and xxvii.

2. Stratfor, "The Geopolitics of the United States, Part 1: The Inevitable Empire," August 24, 2011.

3. Halford J. Mackinder, *Democratic Ideals and Reality* (New York: Henry Holt and Company, 1919; 1942 National Defense University edition), 45–49.

4. The Congressional Budget Office has estimated that according to one scenario, the number of warships could drop to 208 by 2044. "Preserving the Navy's Forward Presence with a Smaller Fleet," March 2015.

5. John Darwin, *After Tamerlane: The Rise and Fall of Global Empires, 1400–2000* (New York: Bloomsbury Press, 2008), 22–23, 236, 469, 479, and 491.

6. Ibid., 469.

7. Paul Kennedy, *Grand Strategies in War and Peace* (New Haven, CT: Yale University Press, 1991), 167.

8. Darwin, *After Tamerlane,* 479.

9. William Pfaff, "Why the Arab World Fights," *The American Conservative,* November/December 2014.

10. Robert D. Kaplan, "America's Imperial Class," Stratfor, November 21, 2012.

11. John Lewis Gaddis, *George F. Kennan: An American Life* (New York: Penguin Press, 2011), 278.

12. Ibid., 299.

13. Bernard DeVoto, *The Course of Empire* (Boston: Houghton Mifflin, 1952), 266.

14. Andrew J. Birtle, *U.S. Army Counterinsurgency and Contingency Operations Doctrine 1860–1941* (Washington, D.C.: Center of Military History, 2004), 7–12.

15. Brian McAllister Linn, *The Echo of Battle: The Army's Way of War* (Cambridge, MA: Harvard University Press, 2007), 71–73.

16. William Pfaff, *The Irony of Manifest Destiny: The Tragedy of America's Foreign Policy* (New York: Walker & Company, 2010), 71–72, 86, and 99–100.

17. Herman Melville, *Moby-Dick* (1851; repr., New York: Knopf, 1988), 576.

18. Charles Olson, *Call Me Ishmael* (San Francisco: City Lights Books, 1947), 12 and 14.

19. Gaddis, *George F. Kennan*, 323 and 435.

INDEX

ABOUT THE AUTHOR

ROBERT D. KAPLAN is the bestselling author of seventeen books on foreign affairs and travel translated into many languages, including *Earning the Rockies, In Europe's Shadow, Asia's Cauldron, The Revenge of Geography, Monsoon, The Coming Anarchy,* and *Balkan Ghosts.* He is a senior fellow at the Center for a New American Security and a senior advisor at Eurasia Group. For three decades his work has appeared in *The Atlantic.* He held the national security chair at the United States Naval Academy and was a member of the Pentagon's Defense Policy Board. *Foreign Policy* magazine twice named him one of the world's Top 100 Global Thinkers.

robertdkaplan.com

cnas.org

ABOUT THE TYPE

This book was set in Requiem, a typeface designed by the Hoefler Type Foundry. It is a modern typeface inspired by inscriptional capitals in Ludovico Vicentino degli Arrighi's 1523 writing manual, *Il modo de temperare le penne*. An original lowercase, a set of figures, and an italic in the chancery style that Arrighi (fl. 1522) helped popularize were created to make this adaptation of a classical design into a complete font family.